GORDON
YAMAMOTO
AND THE KiNG OF THE GEEKS

BY GENE YANG

Published by Amazelnk, a division of SLG Publishing

President/Publisher – Dan Vado
Editor-in-Chief – Jennifer de Guzman
Director of Sales – Deb Moskyok
Production Assistant – Eleanor Lawson

SLG Publishing
P.O. Box 26427
San Jose, CA 95113

Gordon Yamamoto and the King of the Geeks collects issues #1 – 3 of
the series published by Humble Comics.

www.slavelabor.com
www.humblecomics.com

First Printing: May 2004
ISBN 0-943151-95-3

TABLE OF CONTENTS

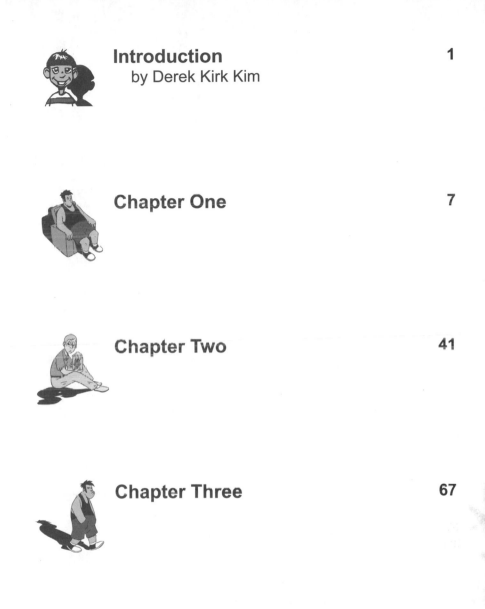

INTRODUCTION
BY DEREK KiRK KiM

Magical.

There are very few works of fiction upon which I could affix that adjective without half a sardonic smirk on my face. *The Little Prince*, *My Neighbor Totoro*, *A Wrinkle In Time* are a few that come immediately to mind. Funny how none of these are comics. How sad, actually. You would think a medium seeping with yarns of flying men, talking animals, rocket ships, vampires, witches and princesses would be filled with nothing but magical stories. But we all know a story isn't made "magical" simply by stuffing it with fairies and magic potions.

Gordon Yamamoto and tho King of the Geeks is that rarest of all breeds — a story that embodies the genuine enthusiasm and boundless imagination of a ten-year-old kid with tho wisdom and craftmanship of a contemplative adult. In an industry where childhood fancies have been manufactured through cold, careful dissection and "market research," Gene Yang doesn't even have to try. It simply flows out of him like battles you waged with your Transformers on a shag carpet back when rushing home to watch cartoons was the highlight of your day.

Although David Copperfield might disagree, Gene is a magician. He tricks you. He messes with your predictions and preconceptions. He clouds your mind with stories insanely fun and addicting to read. Then when you least expect it, he clears away the smoke and lets the themes bubbling under the surface blow up in your face. But it's never painful or didactic, and that's the greatest trick of all. He gently and humbly engages you with everyday issues and struggles that concern all of us: forgiveness, conformity, social hierarchy, and tolerance. All that bookended with a boy shoving a TV cable up his nostril and animal crackers come to manic life.

That's *Gordon Yamamoto and the King of the Geeks*.

That's magical.

Derek Kirk Kim
Same Difference and Other Stories

CHAPTER ONE

1

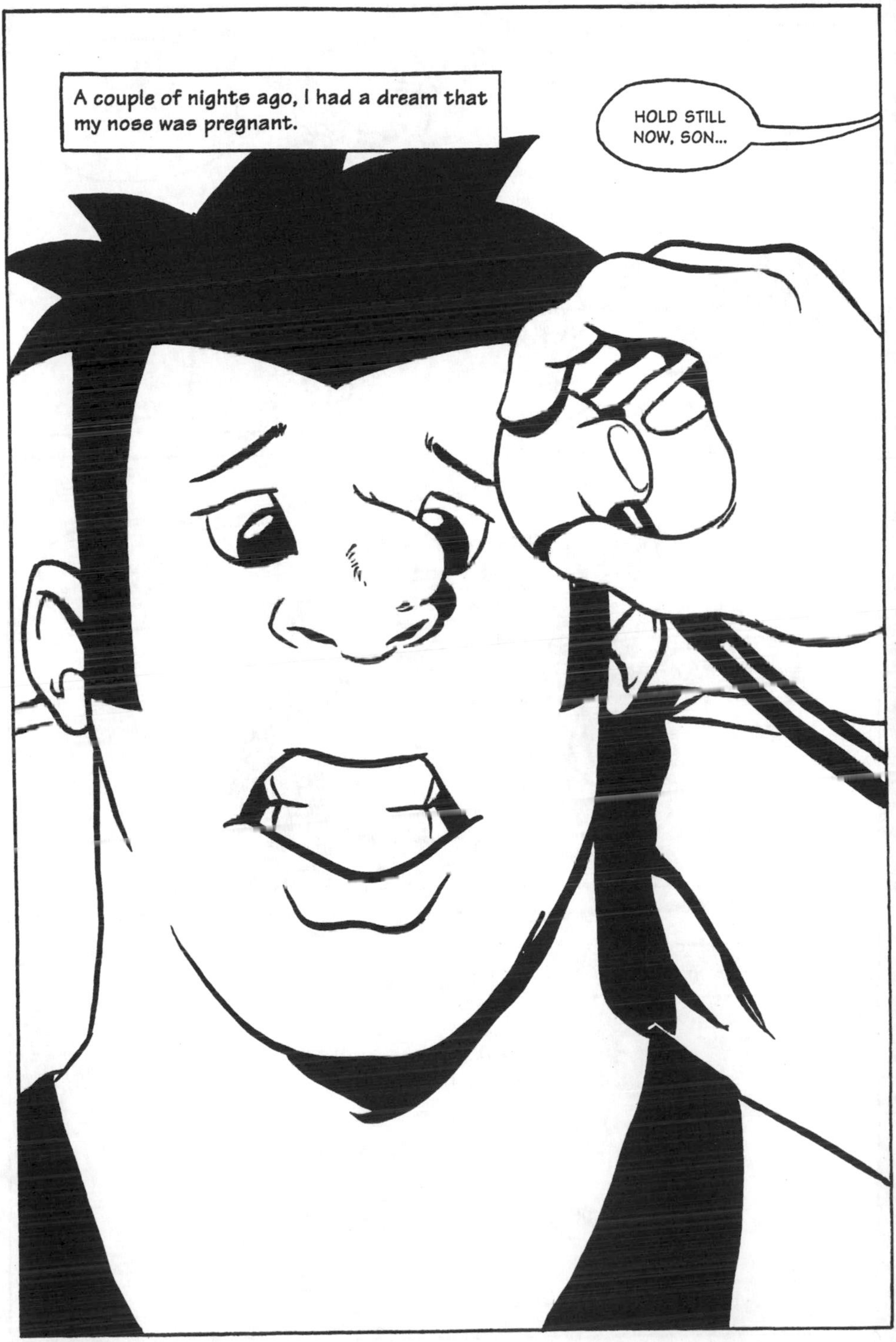
A couple of nights ago, I had a dream that my nose was pregnant.
HOLD STILL NOW, SON...

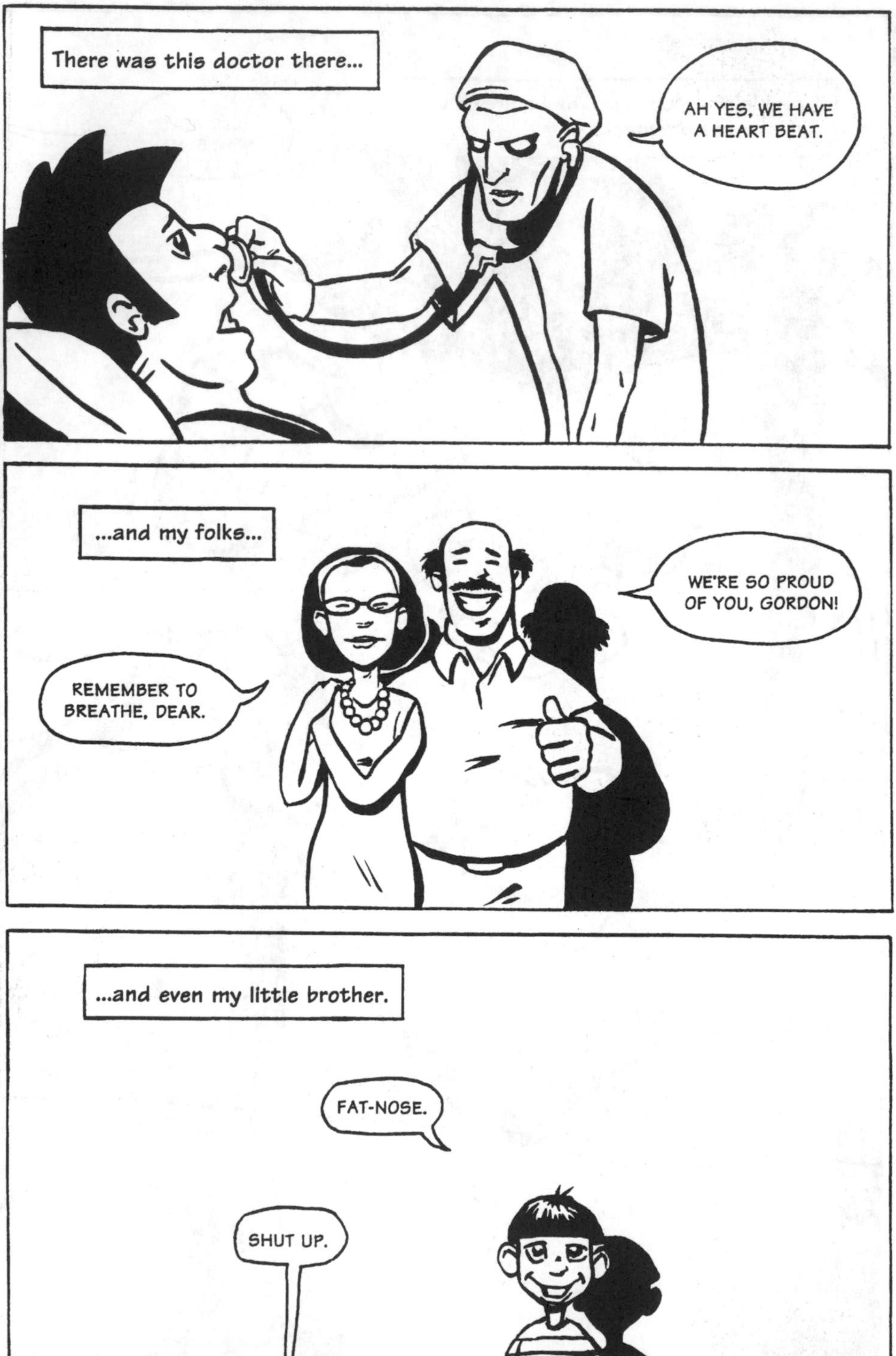
There was this doctor there...
AH YES, WE HAVE A HEART BEAT.
...and my folks...
WE'RE SO PROUD OF YOU, GORDON!
REMEMBER TO BREATHE, DEAR.
...and even my little brother.
FAT-NOSE.
SHUT UP.

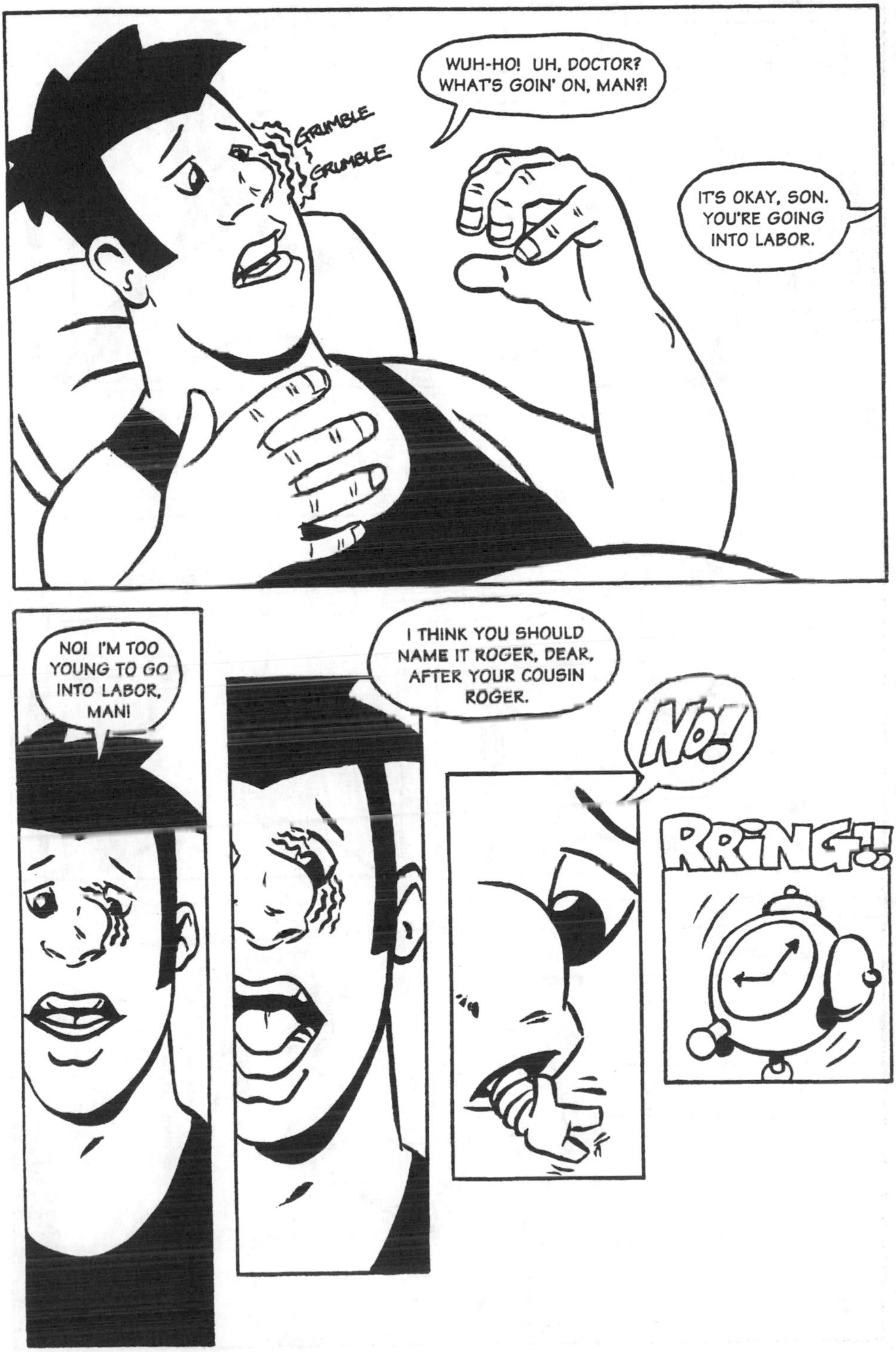
WUH-HO! UH, DOCTOR? WHAT'S GOIN' ON, MAN?!
GRUMBLE GRUMBLE
IT'S OKAY, SON. YOU'RE GOING INTO LABOR.
NO! I'M TOO YOUNG TO GO INTO LABOR, MAN!
I THINK YOU SHOULD NAME IT ROGER, DEAR, AFTER YOUR COUSIN ROGER.
NO!
RRING!!

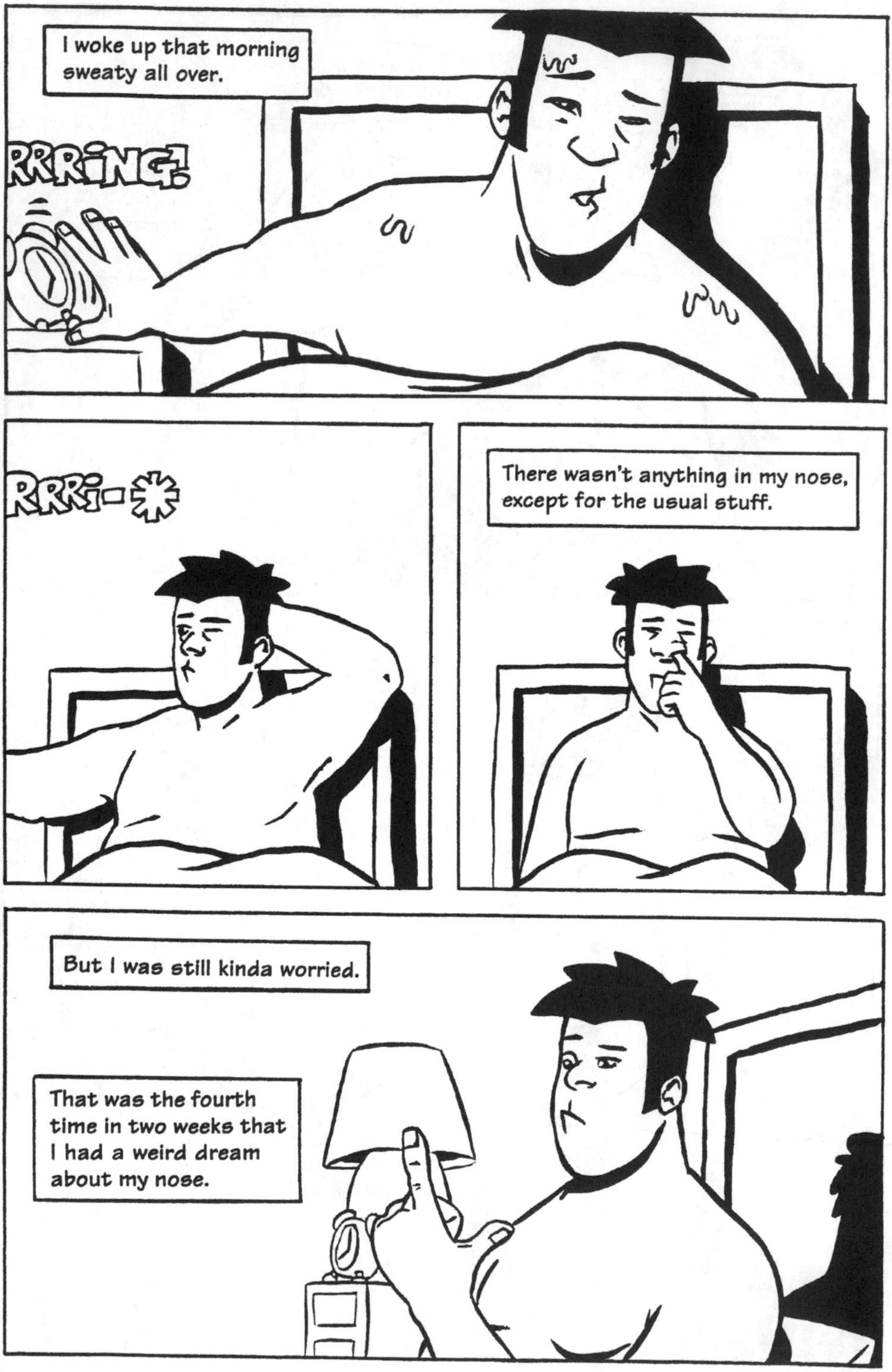
I woke up that morning sweaty all over.
RRRING!
RRRi-
There wasn't anything in my nose, except for the usual stuff.
But I was still kinda worried.
That was the fourth time in two weeks that I had a weird dream about my nose.

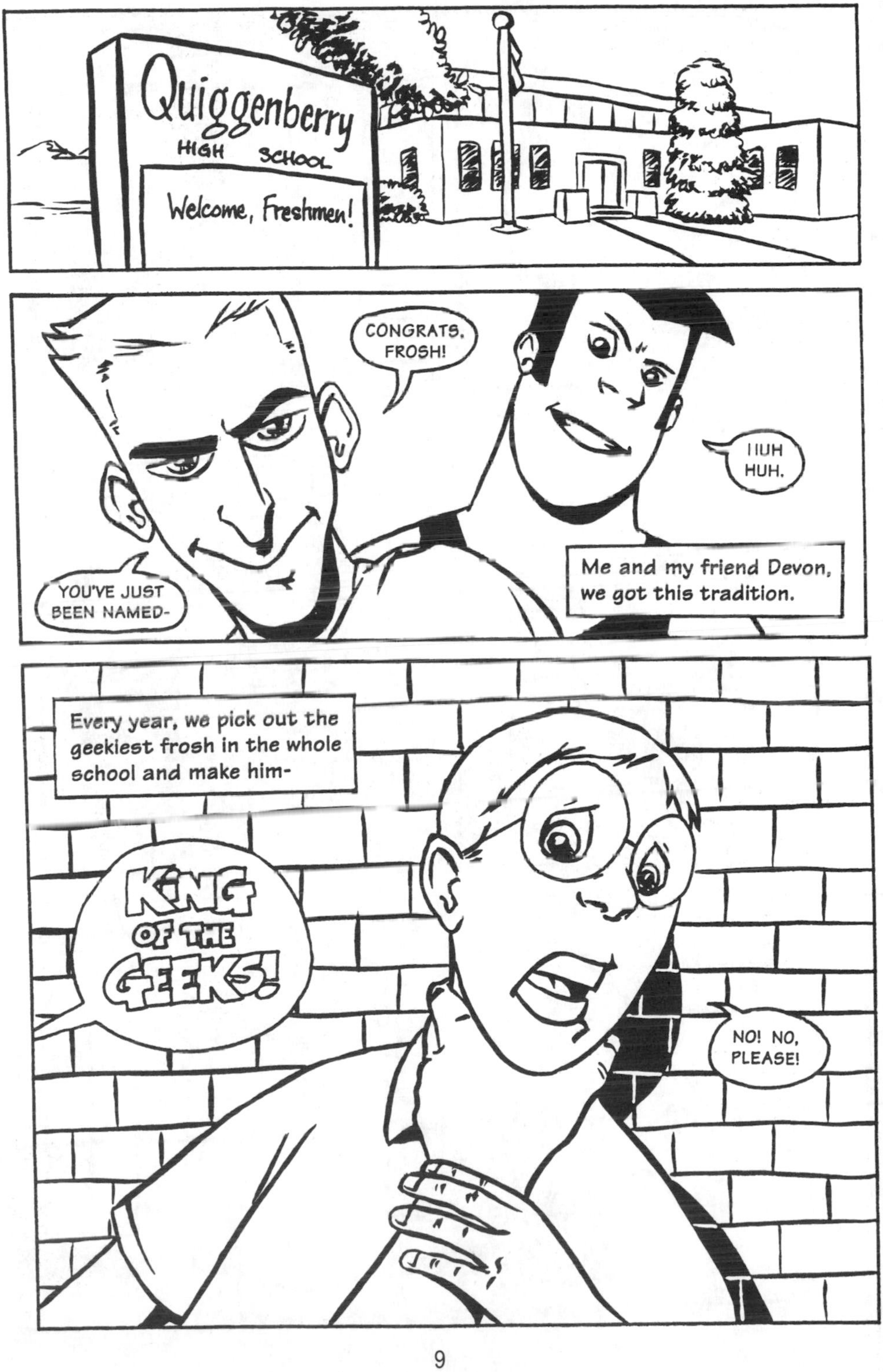
Quiggenberry
HIGH SCHOOL
Welcome, Freshmen!
CONGRATS, FROSH!
YOU'VE JUST BEEN NAMED-
HUH HUH.
Me and my friend Devon, we got this tradition.
Every year, we pick out the geekiest frosh in the whole school and make him-
KING OF THE GEEKS!
NO! NO, PLEASE!

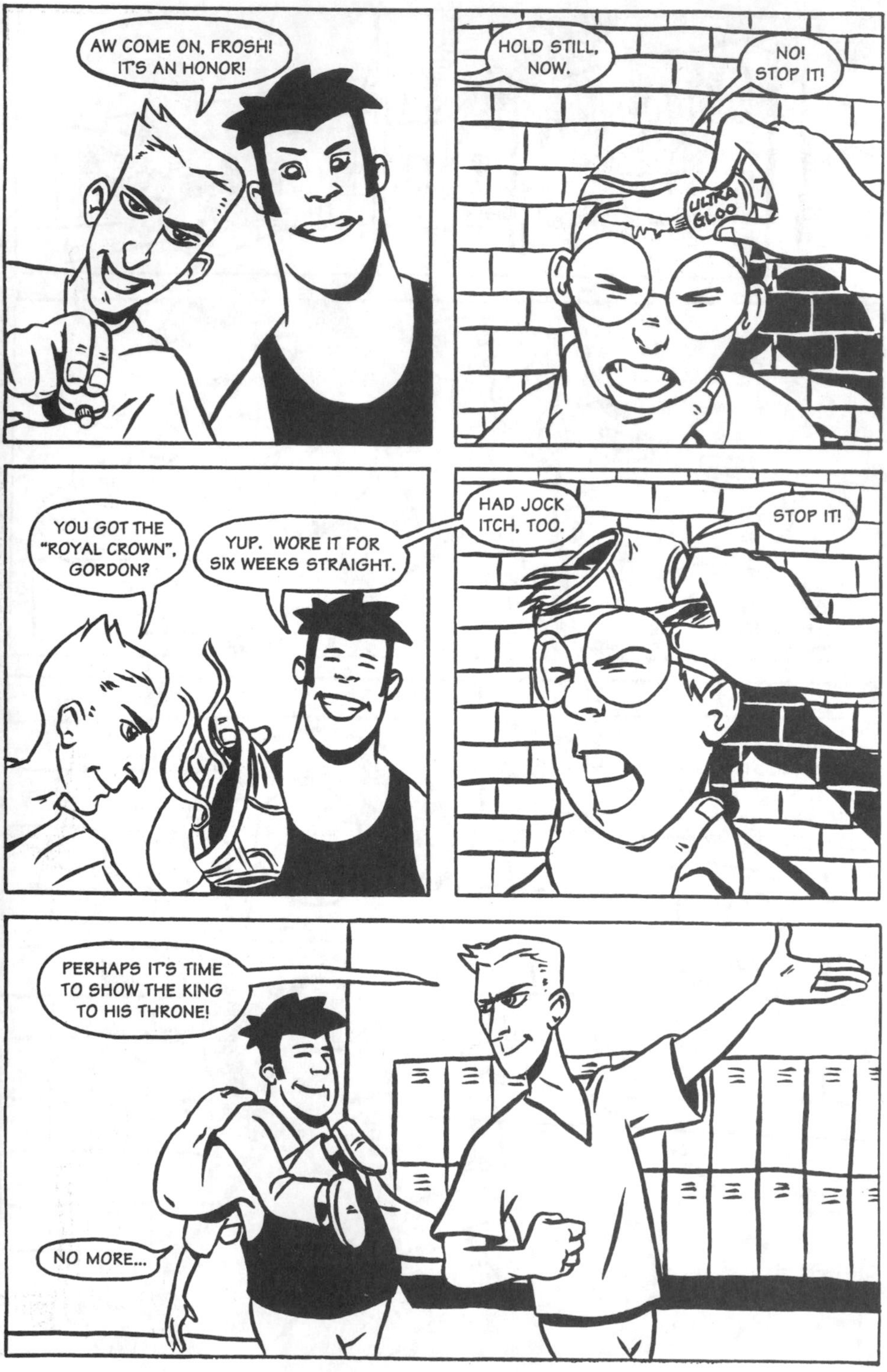
AW COME ON, FROSH! IT'S AN HONOR!
HOLD STILL, NOW.
NO! STOP IT!
ULTRA GLOO
YOU GOT THE "ROYAL CROWN", GORDON?
YUP. WORE IT FOR SIX WEEKS STRAIGHT.
HAD JOCK ITCH, TOO.
STOP IT!
PERHAPS IT'S TIME TO SHOW THE KING TO HIS THRONE!
NO MORE...

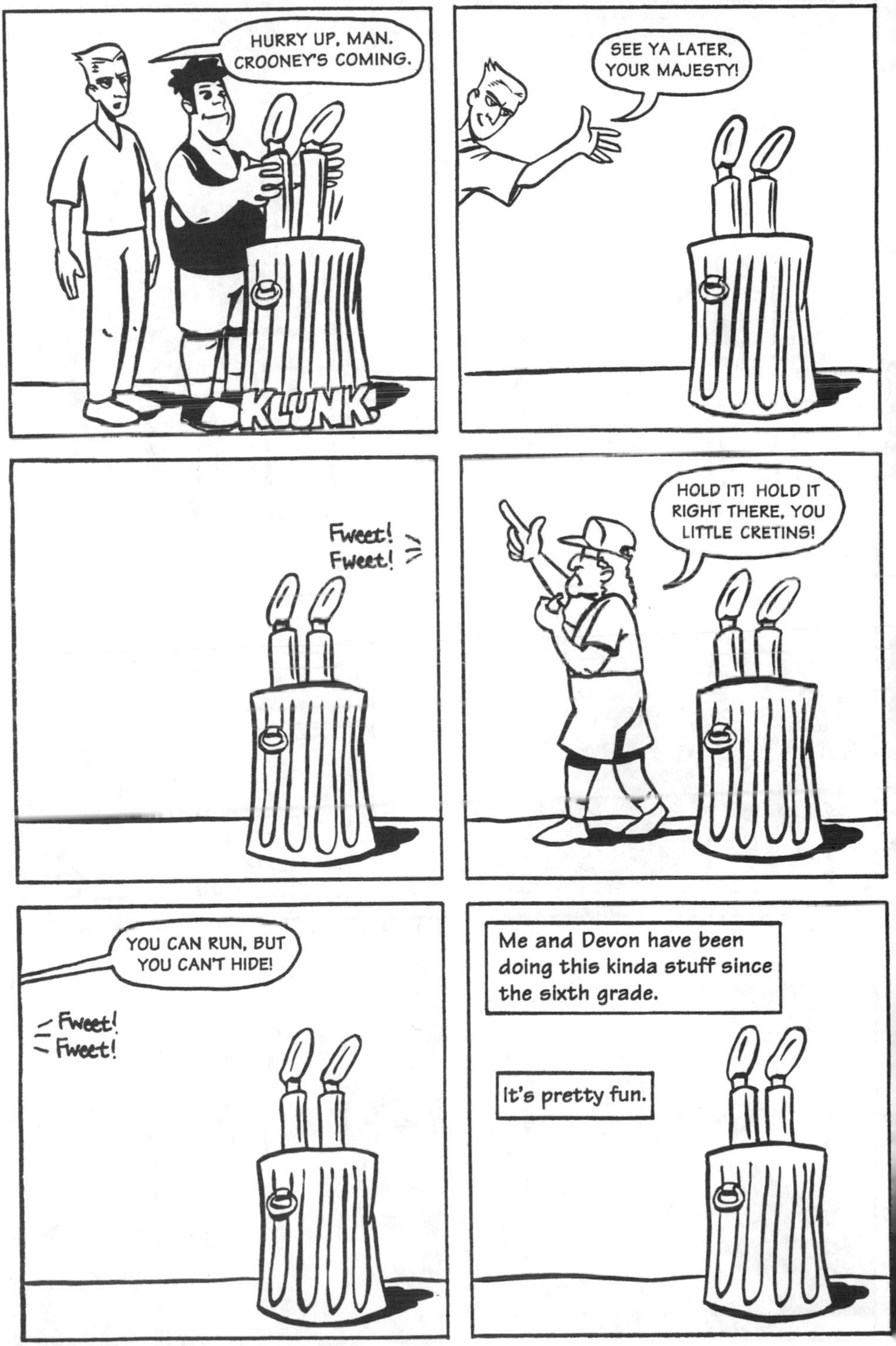
HURRY UP, MAN. CROONEY'S COMING.
KLUNK!
SEE YA LATER, YOUR MAJESTY!
Fweet! Fweet!
HOLD IT! HOLD IT RIGHT THERE, YOU LITTLE CRETINS!
YOU CAN RUN, BUT YOU CAN'T HIDE!
Fweet! Fweet!
Me and Devon have been doing this kinda stuff since the sixth grade.
It's pretty fun.

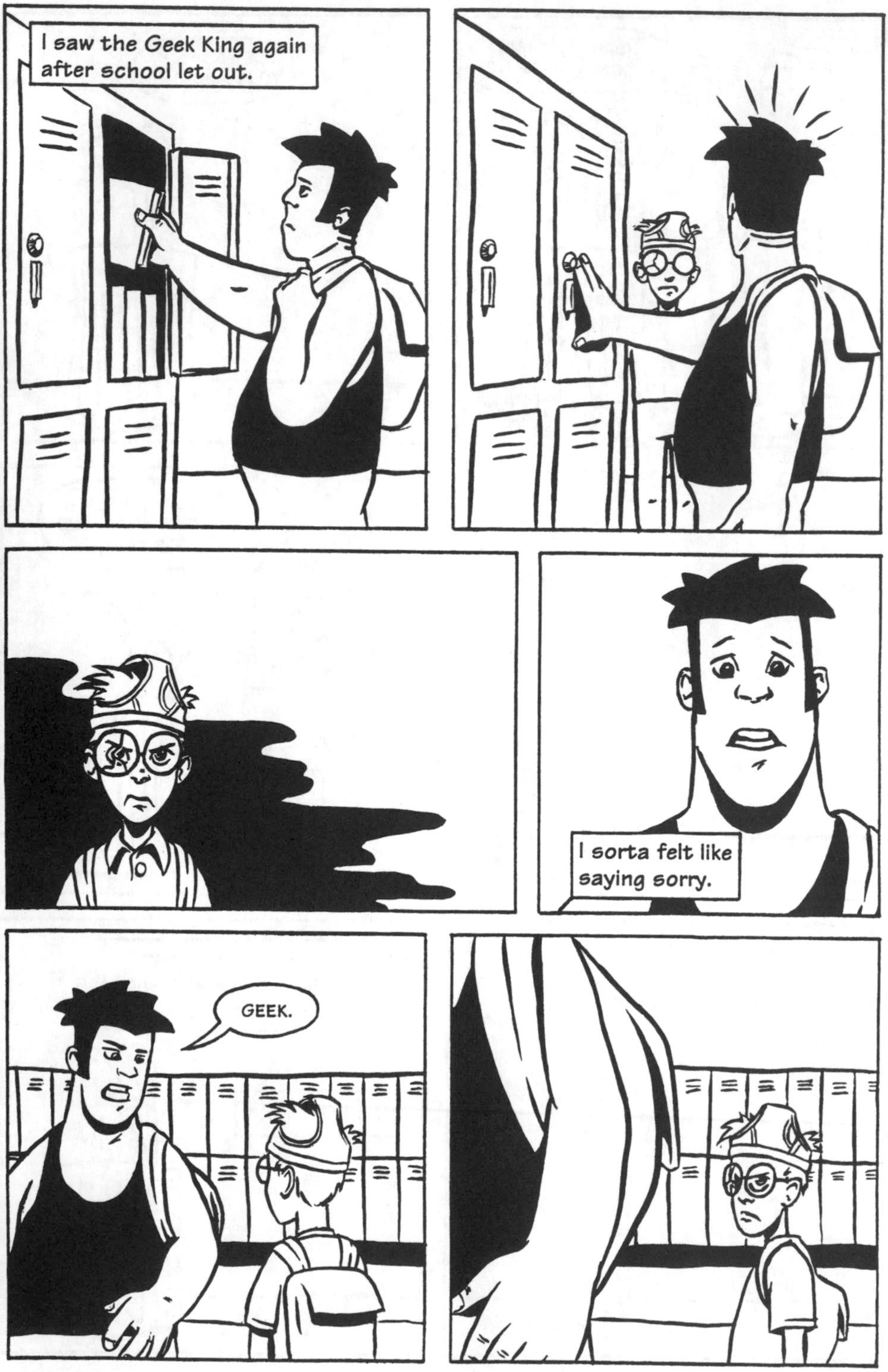
I saw the Geek King again
after school let out.
I sorta felt like
saying sorry.
GEEK.

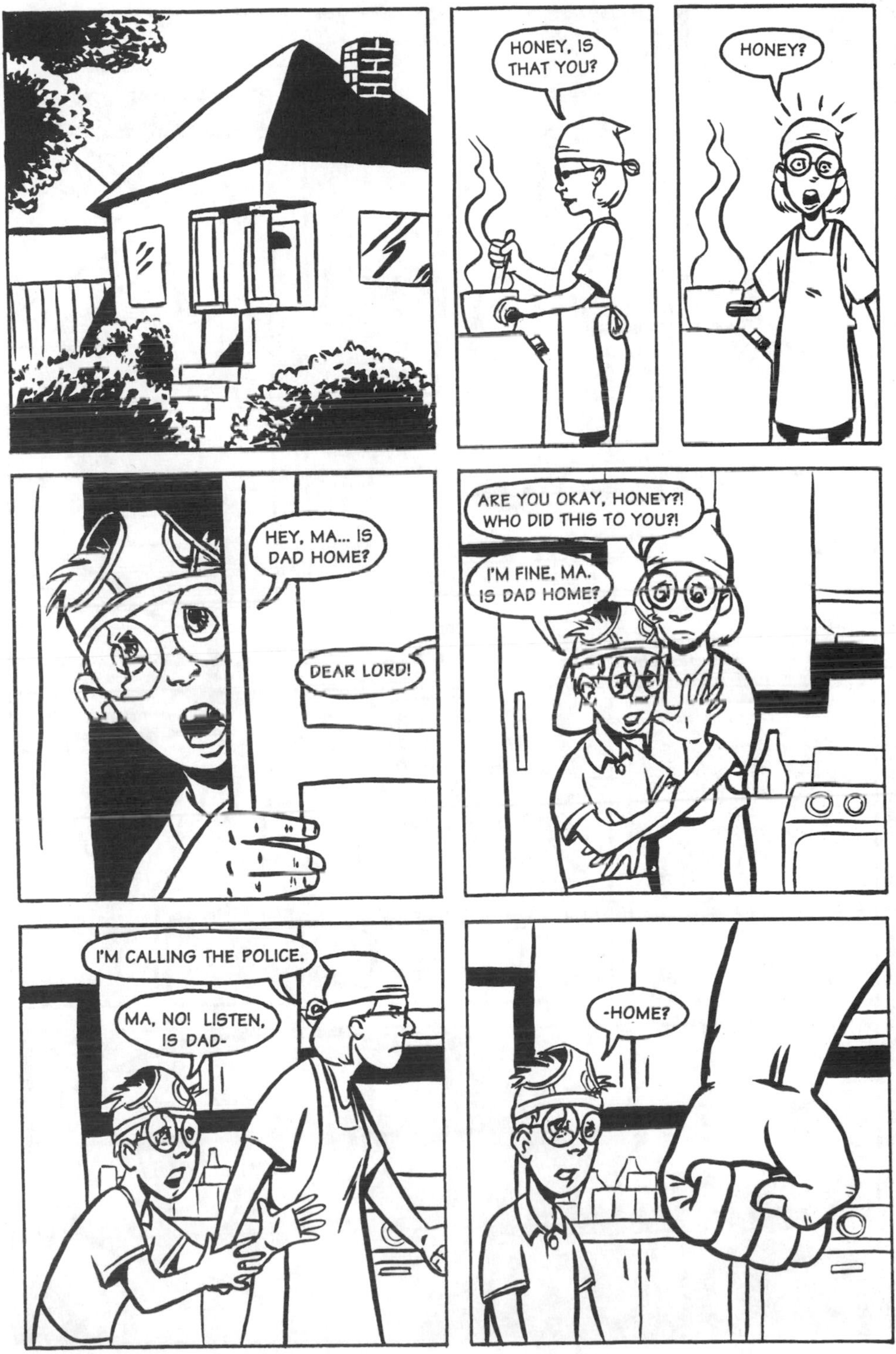
HONEY, IS THAT YOU?
HONEY?
HEY, MA... IS DAD HOME?
DEAR LORD!
ARE YOU OKAY, HONEY?! WHO DID THIS TO YOU?!
I'M FINE, MA. IS DAD HOME?
I'M CALLING THE POLICE.
MA, NO! LISTEN, IS DAD-
-HOME?

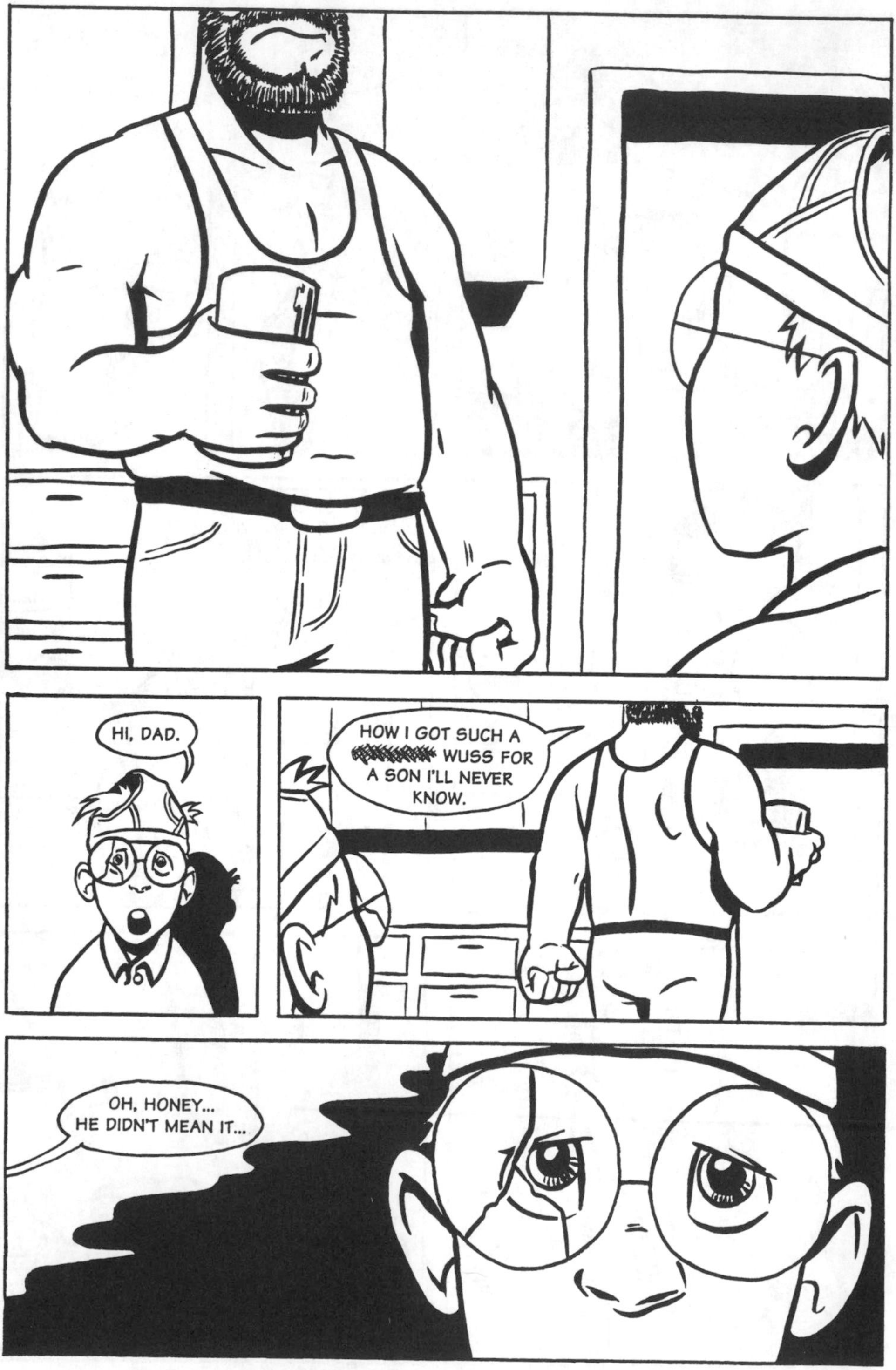
HI, DAD.
HOW I GOT SUCH A [redacted] WUSS FOR A SON I'LL NEVER KNOW.
OH, HONEY... HE DIDN'T MEAN IT...

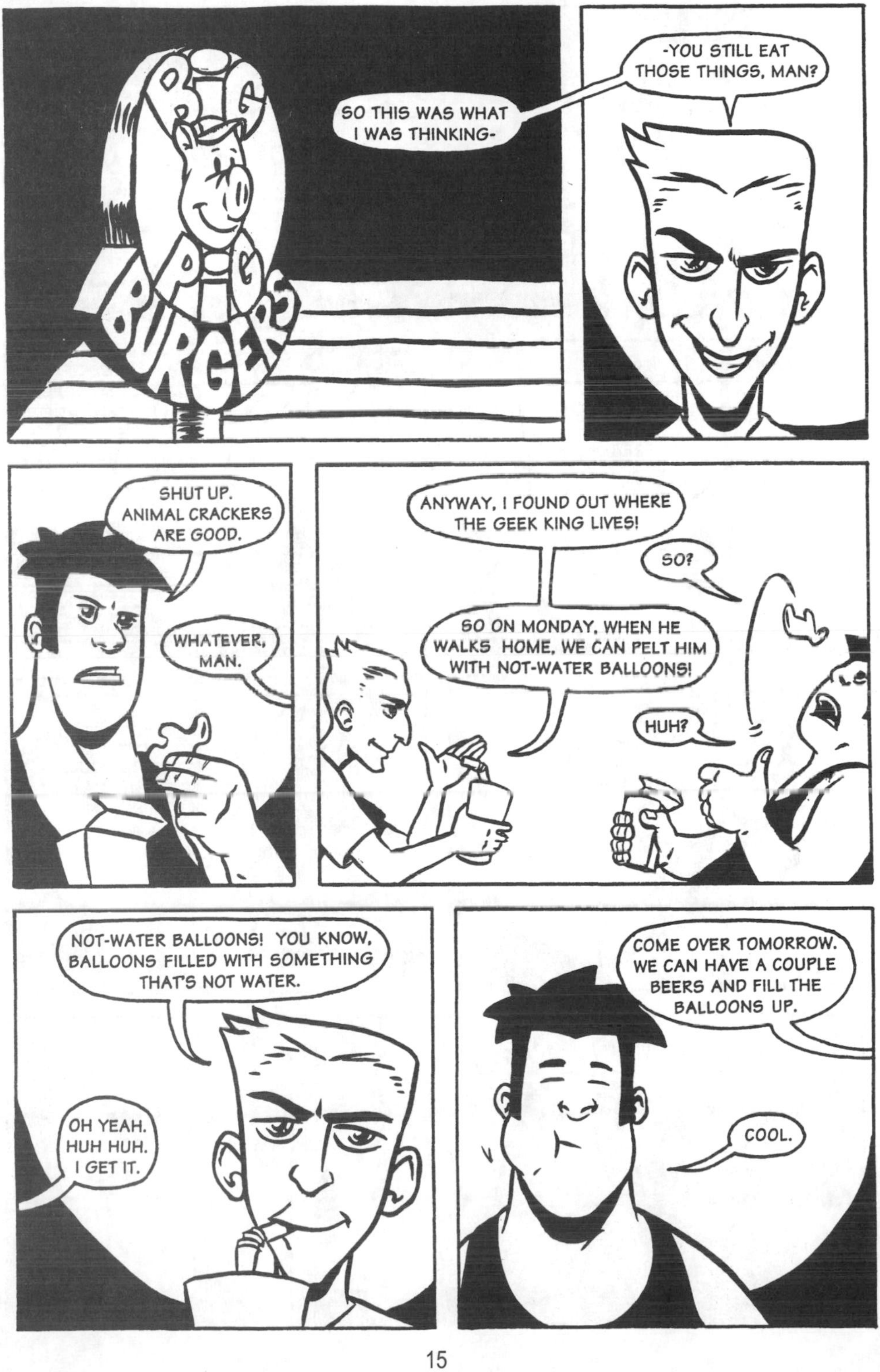
BIG PIG BURGERS
SO THIS WAS WHAT I WAS THINKING-
-YOU STILL EAT THOSE THINGS, MAN?
SHUT UP. ANIMAL CRACKERS ARE GOOD.
WHATEVER, MAN.
ANYWAY, I FOUND OUT WHERE THE GEEK KING LIVES!
SO?
SO ON MONDAY, WHEN HE WALKS HOME, WE CAN PELT HIM WITH NOT-WATER BALLOONS!
HUH?
NOT-WATER BALLOONS! YOU KNOW, BALLOONS FILLED WITH SOMETHING THAT'S NOT WATER.
OH YEAH. HUH HUH. I GET IT.
COME OVER TOMORROW. WE CAN HAVE A COUPLE BEERS AND FILL THE BALLOONS UP.
COOL.

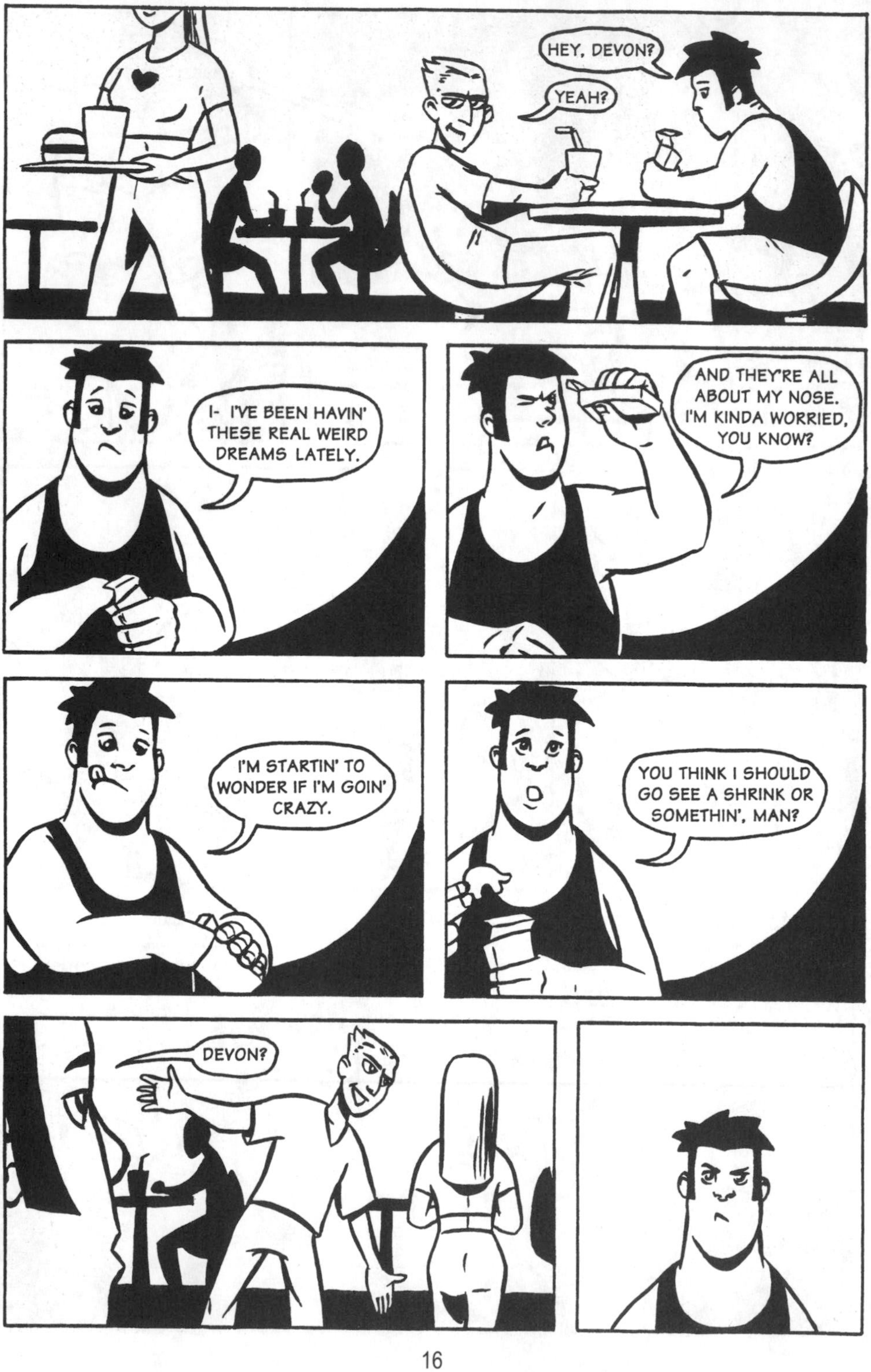
HEY, DEVON?
YEAH?
I- I'VE BEEN HAVIN' THESE REAL WEIRD DREAMS LATELY.
AND THEY'RE ALL ABOUT MY NOSE. I'M KINDA WORRIED, YOU KNOW?
I'M STARTIN' TO WONDER IF I'M GOIN' CRAZY.
YOU THINK I SHOULD GO SEE A SHRINK OR SOMETHIN', MAN?
DEVON?

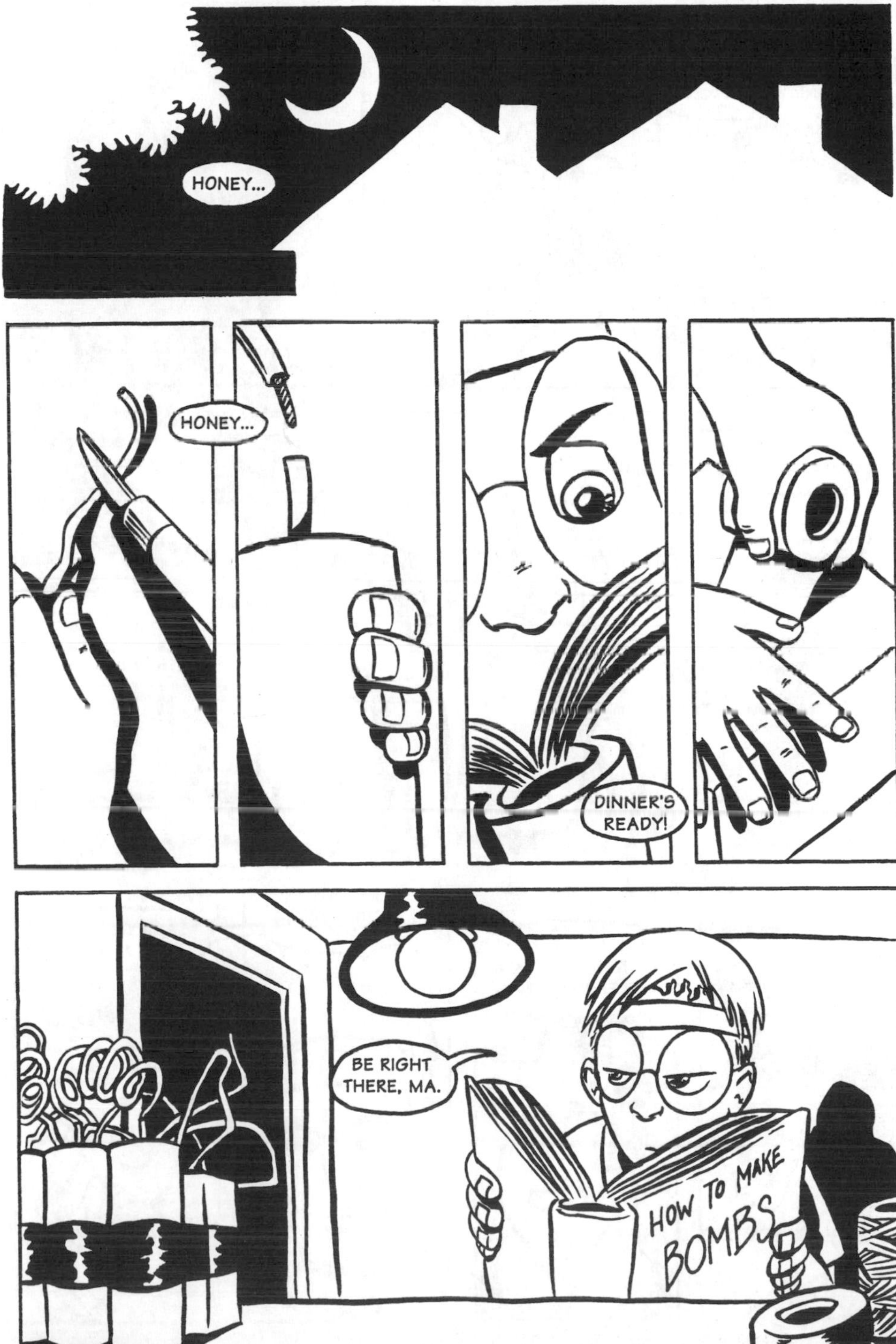
HONEY...
HONEY...
DINNER'S READY!
BE RIGHT THERE, MA.
HOW TO MAKE BOMBS

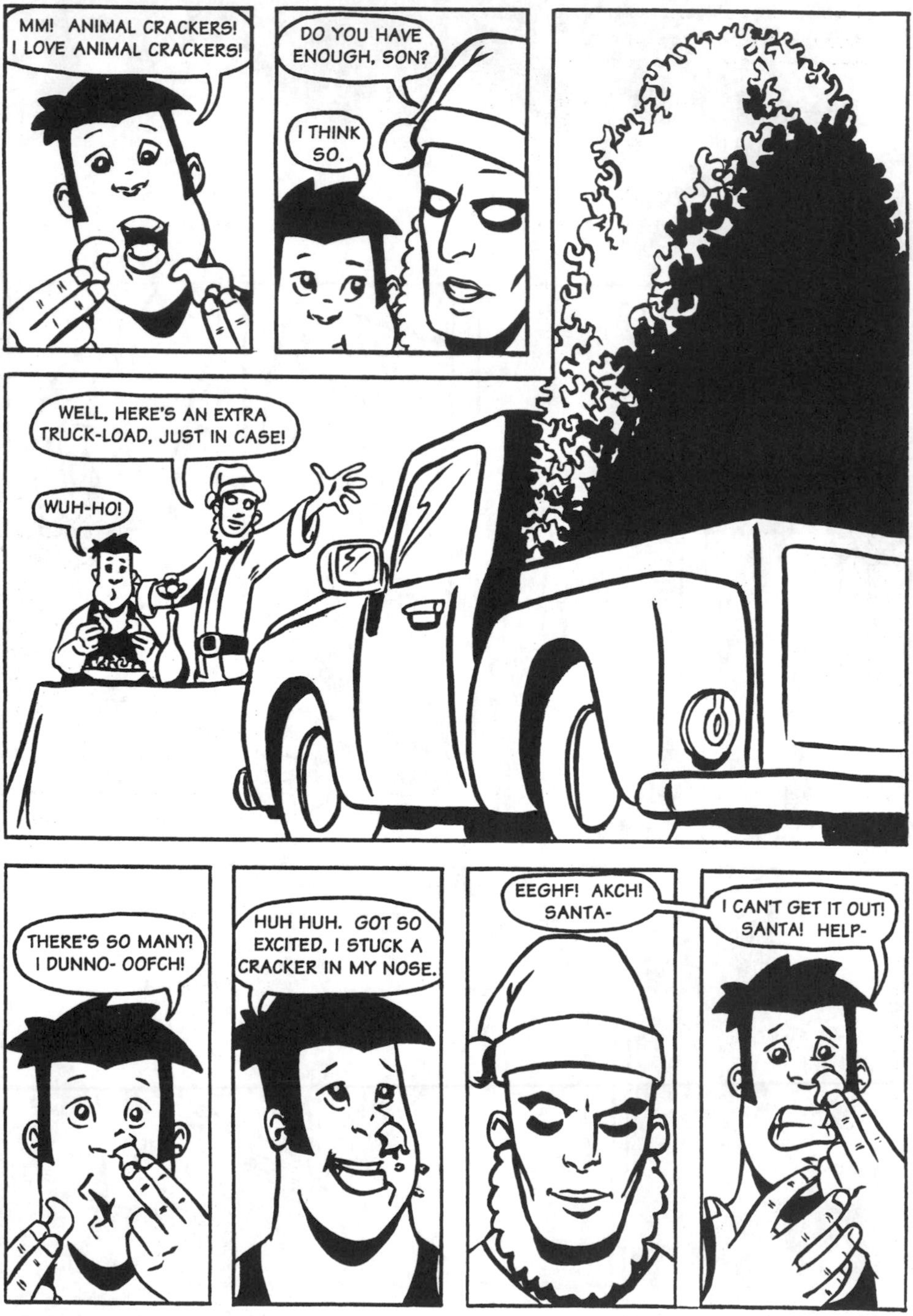
MM! ANIMAL CRACKERS! I LOVE ANIMAL CRACKERS!
DO YOU HAVE ENOUGH, SON?
I THINK SO.
WELL, HERE'S AN EXTRA TRUCK-LOAD, JUST IN CASE!
WUH-HO!
THERE'S SO MANY! I DUNNO- OOFCH!
HUH HUH. GOT SO EXCITED, I STUCK A CRACKER IN MY NOSE.
EEGHF! AKCH! SANTA-
I CAN'T GET IT OUT! SANTA! HELP-

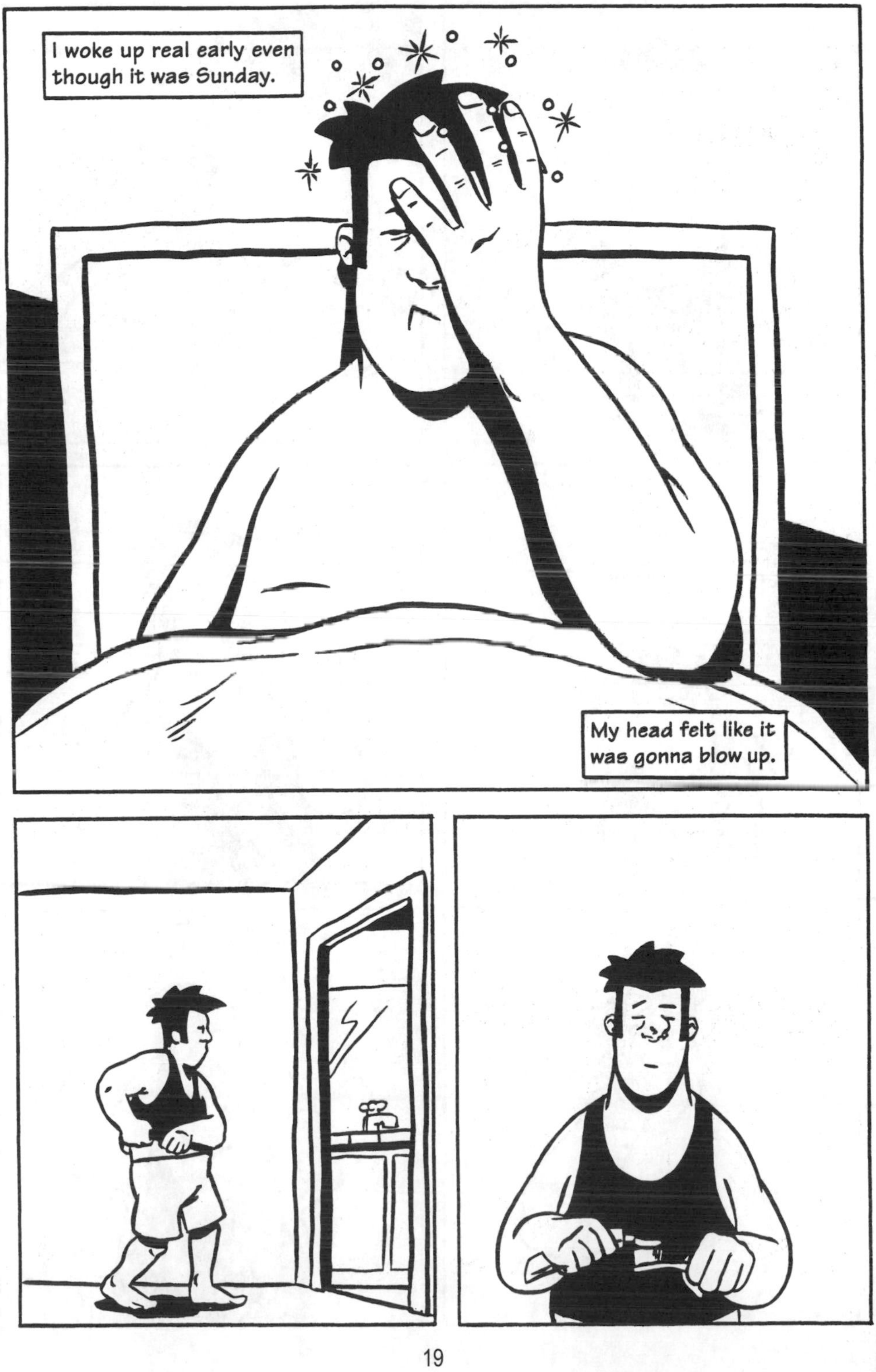
I woke up real early even though it was Sunday.
My head felt like it was gonna blow up.

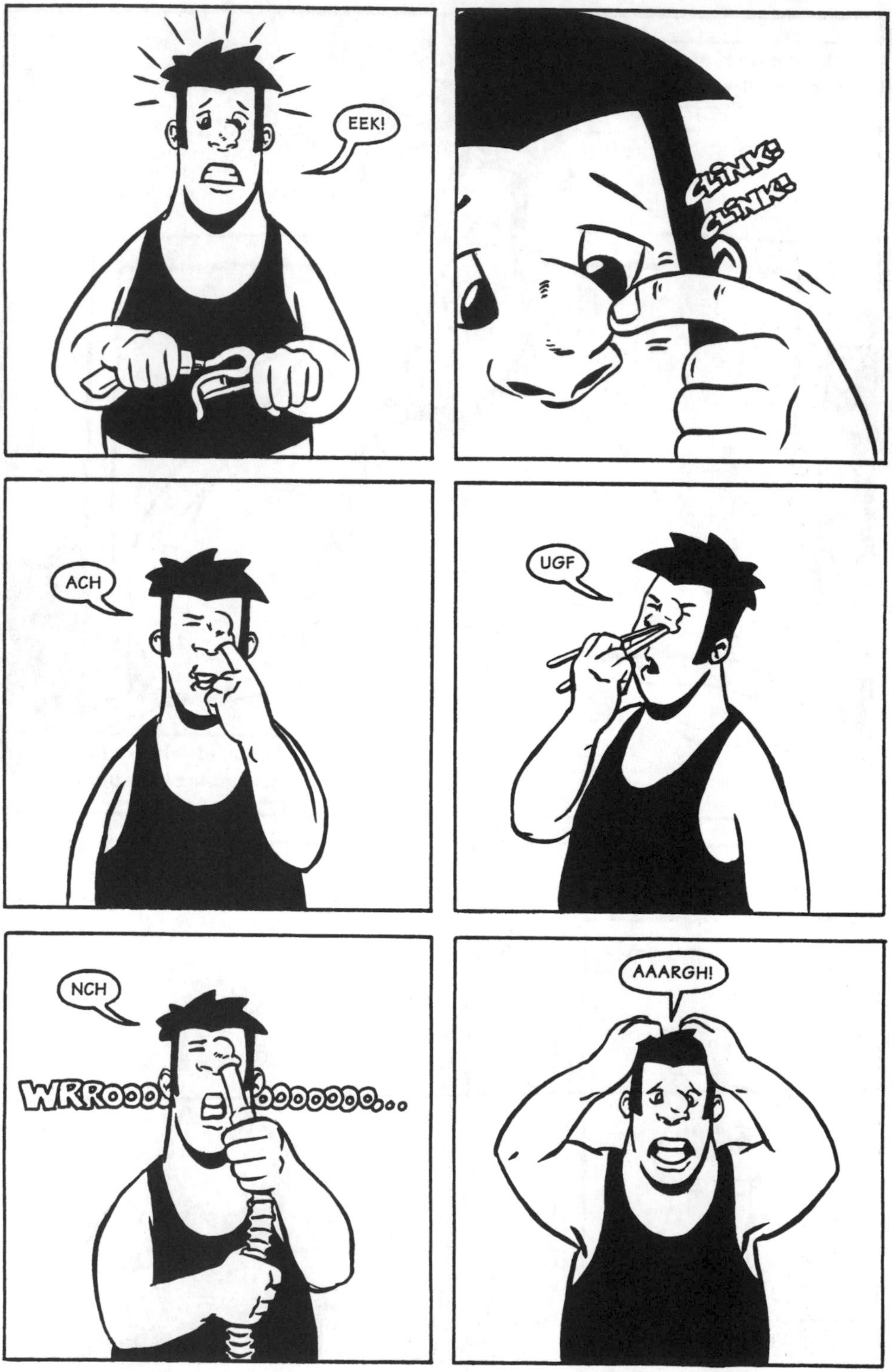
EEK!
CLINK!
CLINK!
ACH
UGF
NCH
WRROOOO
OOOOOOOO...
AAARGH!

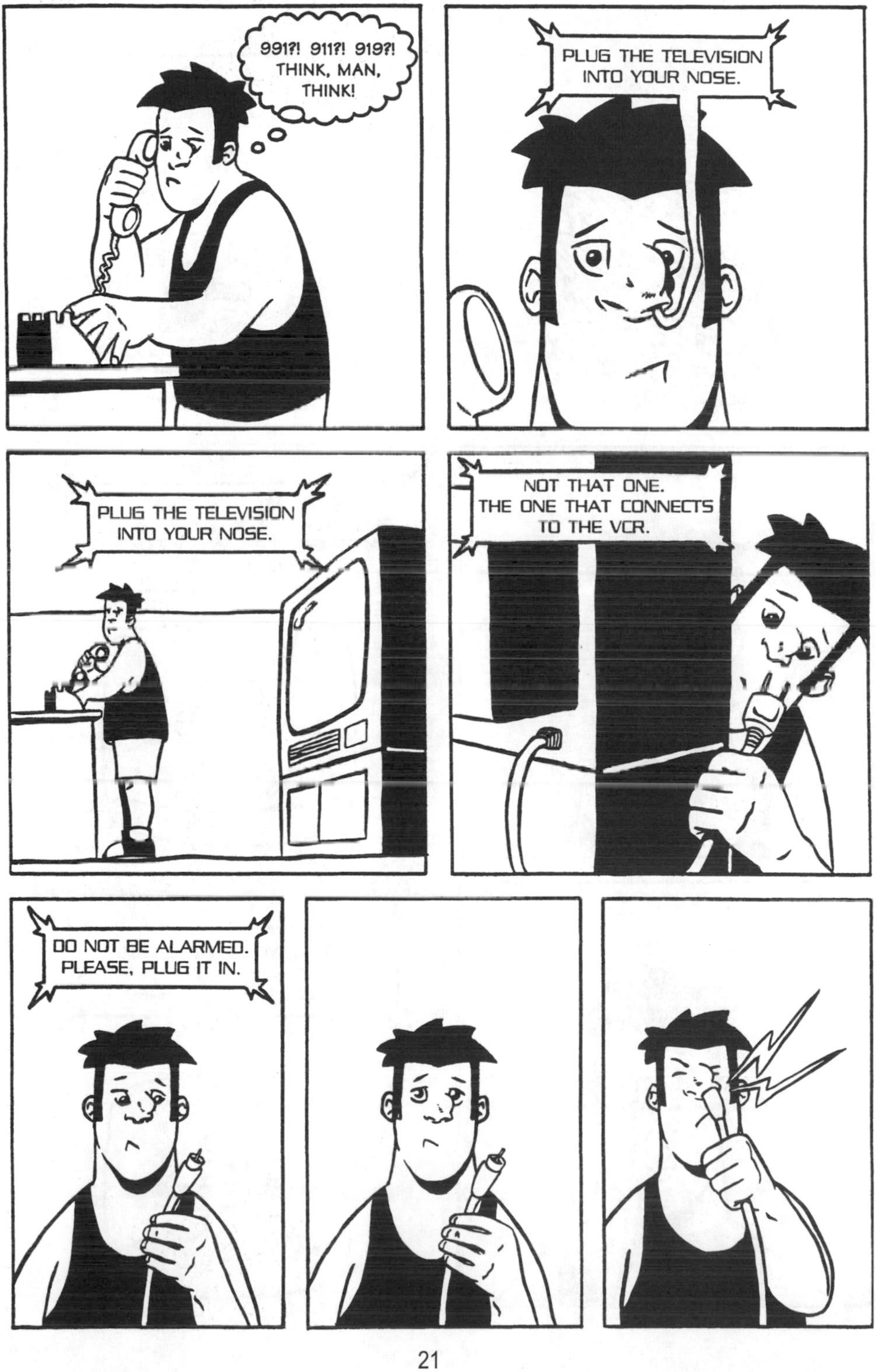
991?! 911?! 919?! THINK, MAN, THINK!
PLUG THE TELEVISION INTO YOUR NOSE.
PLUG THE TELEVISION INTO YOUR NOSE.
NOT THAT ONE. THE ONE THAT CONNECTS TO THE VCR.
DO NOT BE ALARMED. PLEASE, PLUG IT IN.

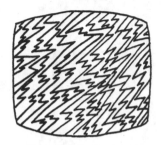

ZZZZT...

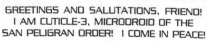

GREETINGS AND SALUTATIONS, FRIEND!
I AM CUTICLE-3, MICRODROID OF THE
SAN PELIGRAN ORDER! I COME IN PEACE!

MY SHIP AND I ARE CURRENTLY
DECAPACITATED IN YOUR SINUSES.
I APOLOGIZE FOR ANY DISCOMFORT
YOU MAY FEEL.

FRIEND, YOU SEEM... TENSE.
PERHAPS A BIT OF EXPLANATION
WILL PUT YOU AT EASE.

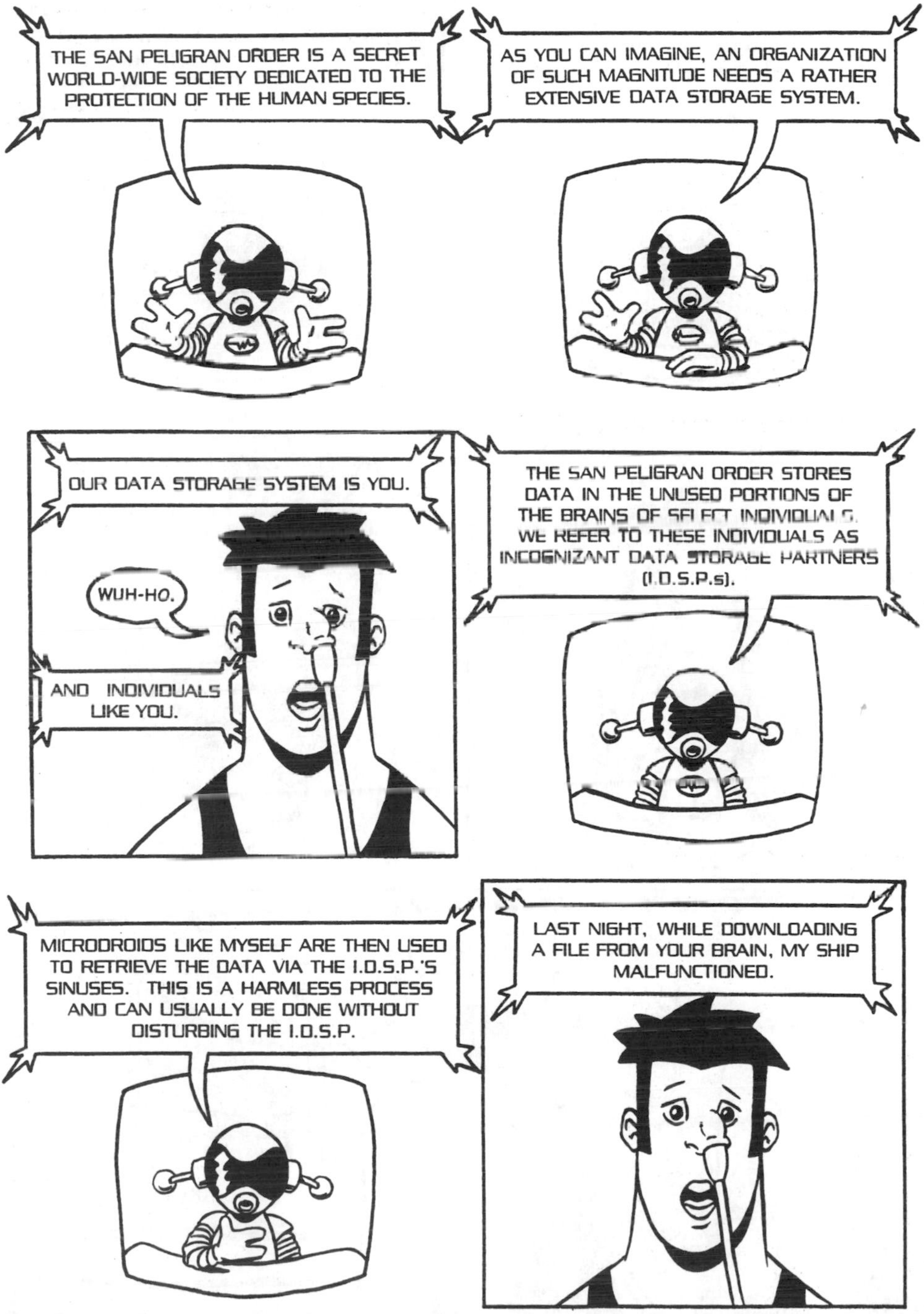
THE SAN PELIGRAN ORDER IS A SECRET WORLD-WIDE SOCIETY DEDICATED TO THE PROTECTION OF THE HUMAN SPECIES.
AS YOU CAN IMAGINE, AN ORGANIZATION OF SUCH MAGNITUDE NEEDS A RATHER EXTENSIVE DATA STORAGE SYSTEM.
OUR DATA STORAGE SYSTEM IS YOU.
WUH-HO.
AND INDIVIDUALS LIKE YOU.
THE SAN PELIGRAN ORDER STORES DATA IN THE UNUSED PORTIONS OF THE BRAINS OF SELECT INDIVIDUALS. WE REFER TO THESE INDIVIDUALS AS INCOGNIZANT DATA STORAGE PARTNERS (I.D.S.P.s).
MICRODROIDS LIKE MYSELF ARE THEN USED TO RETRIEVE THE DATA VIA THE I.D.S.P.'S SINUSES. THIS IS A HARMLESS PROCESS AND CAN USUALLY BE DONE WITHOUT DISTURBING THE I.D.S.P.
LAST NIGHT, WHILE DOWNLOADING A FILE FROM YOUR BRAIN, MY SHIP MALFUNCTIONED.

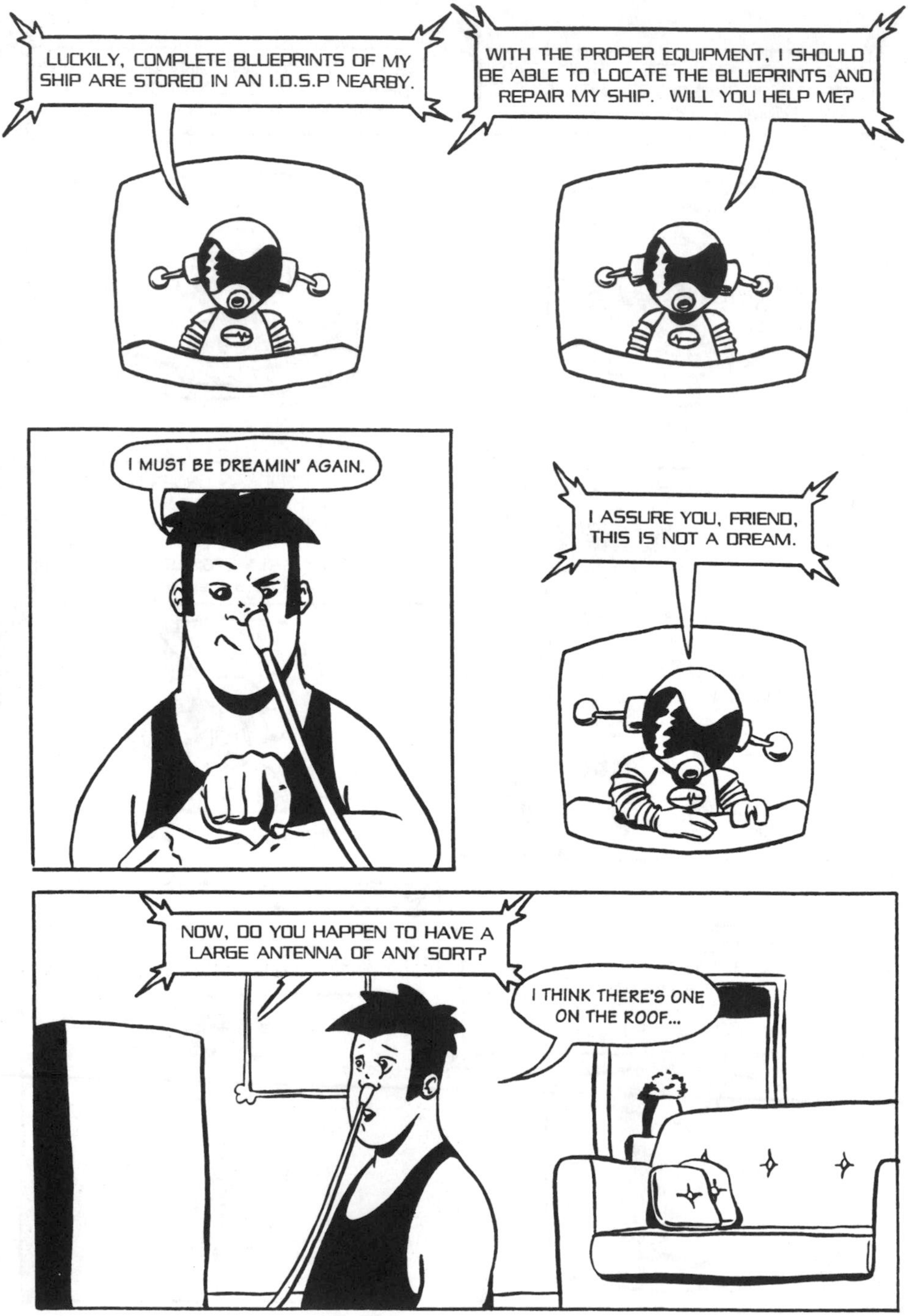
LUCKILY, COMPLETE BLUEPRINTS OF MY SHIP ARE STORED IN AN I.D.S.P NEARBY.
WITH THE PROPER EQUIPMENT, I SHOULD BE ABLE TO LOCATE THE BLUEPRINTS AND REPAIR MY SHIP. WILL YOU HELP ME?
I MUST BE DREAMIN' AGAIN.
I ASSURE YOU, FRIEND, THIS IS NOT A DREAM.
NOW, DO YOU HAPPEN TO HAVE A LARGE ANTENNA OF ANY SORT?
I THINK THERE'S ONE ON THE ROOF...

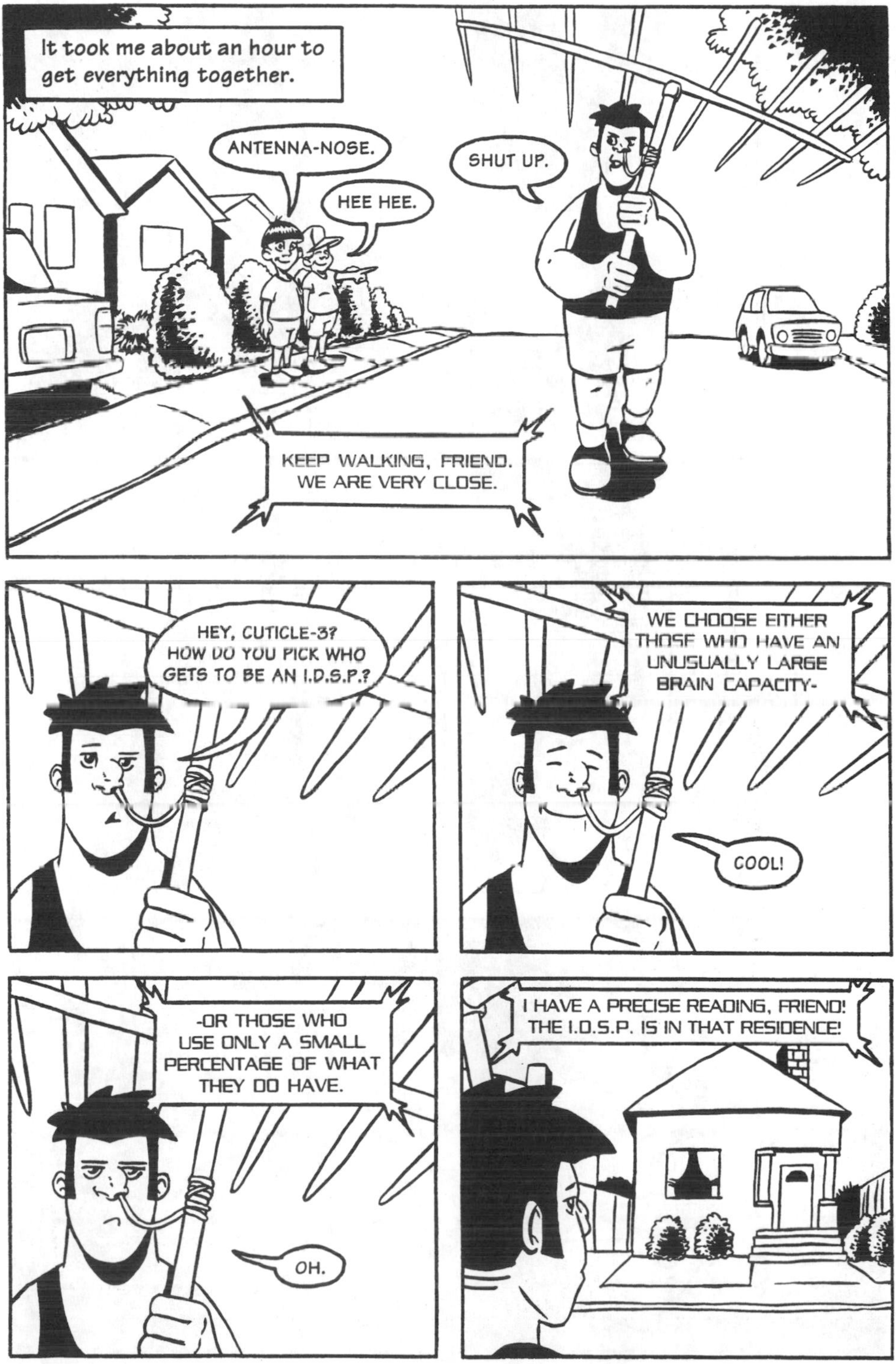
It took me about an hour to get everything together.
ANTENNA-NOSE.
HEE HEE.
SHUT UP.
KEEP WALKING, FRIEND. WE ARE VERY CLOSE.
HEY, CUTICLE-3? HOW DO YOU PICK WHO GETS TO BE AN I.D.S.P.?
WE CHOOSE EITHER THOSE WHO HAVE AN UNUSUALLY LARGE BRAIN CAPACITY-
COOL!
-OR THOSE WHO USE ONLY A SMALL PERCENTAGE OF WHAT THEY DO HAVE.
OH.
I HAVE A PRECISE READING, FRIEND! THE I.D.S.P. IS IN THAT RESIDENCE!

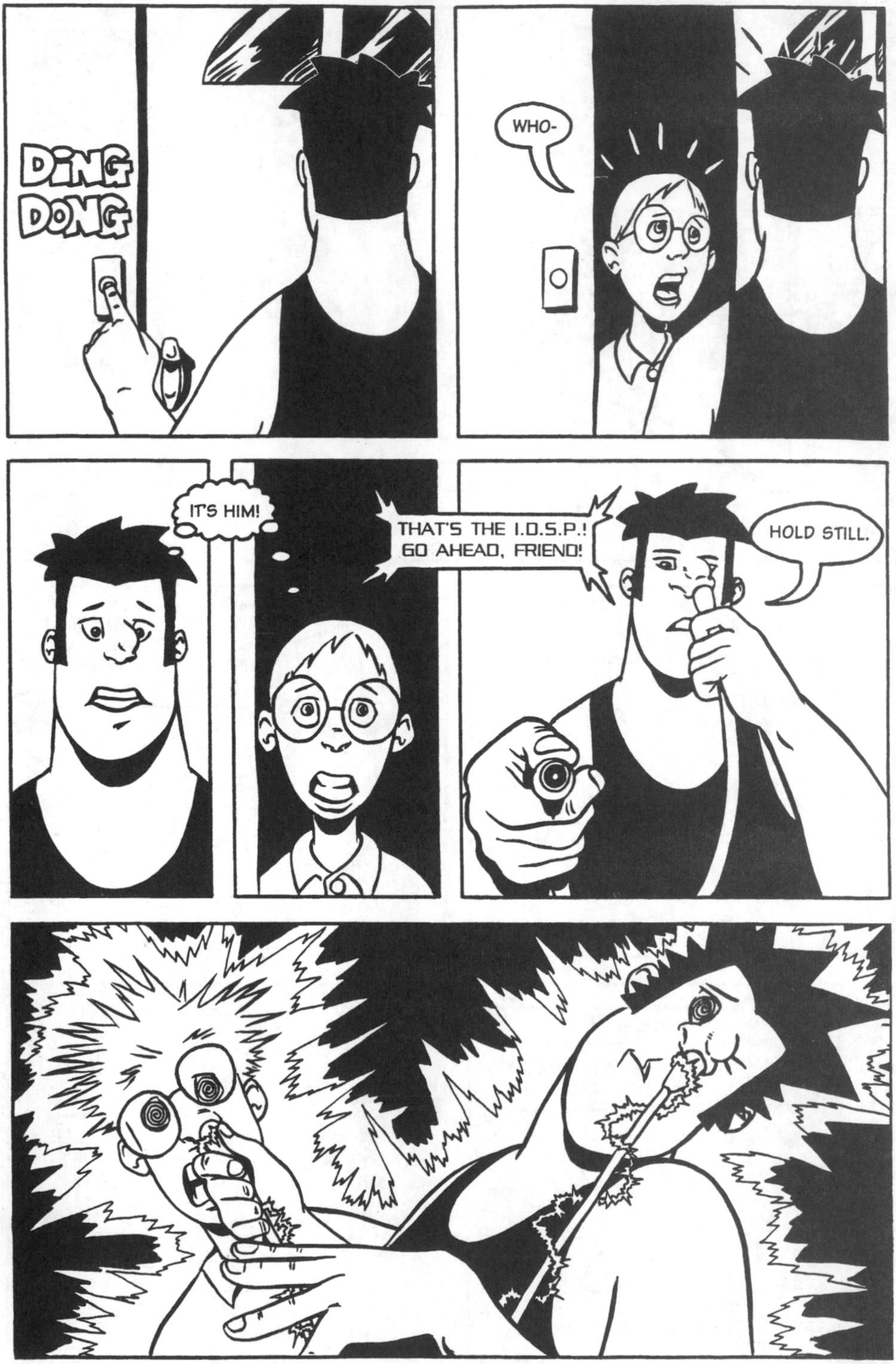
DING DONG
WHO-
IT'S HIM!
THAT'S THE I.D.S.P.! GO AHEAD, FRIEND!
HOLD STILL.

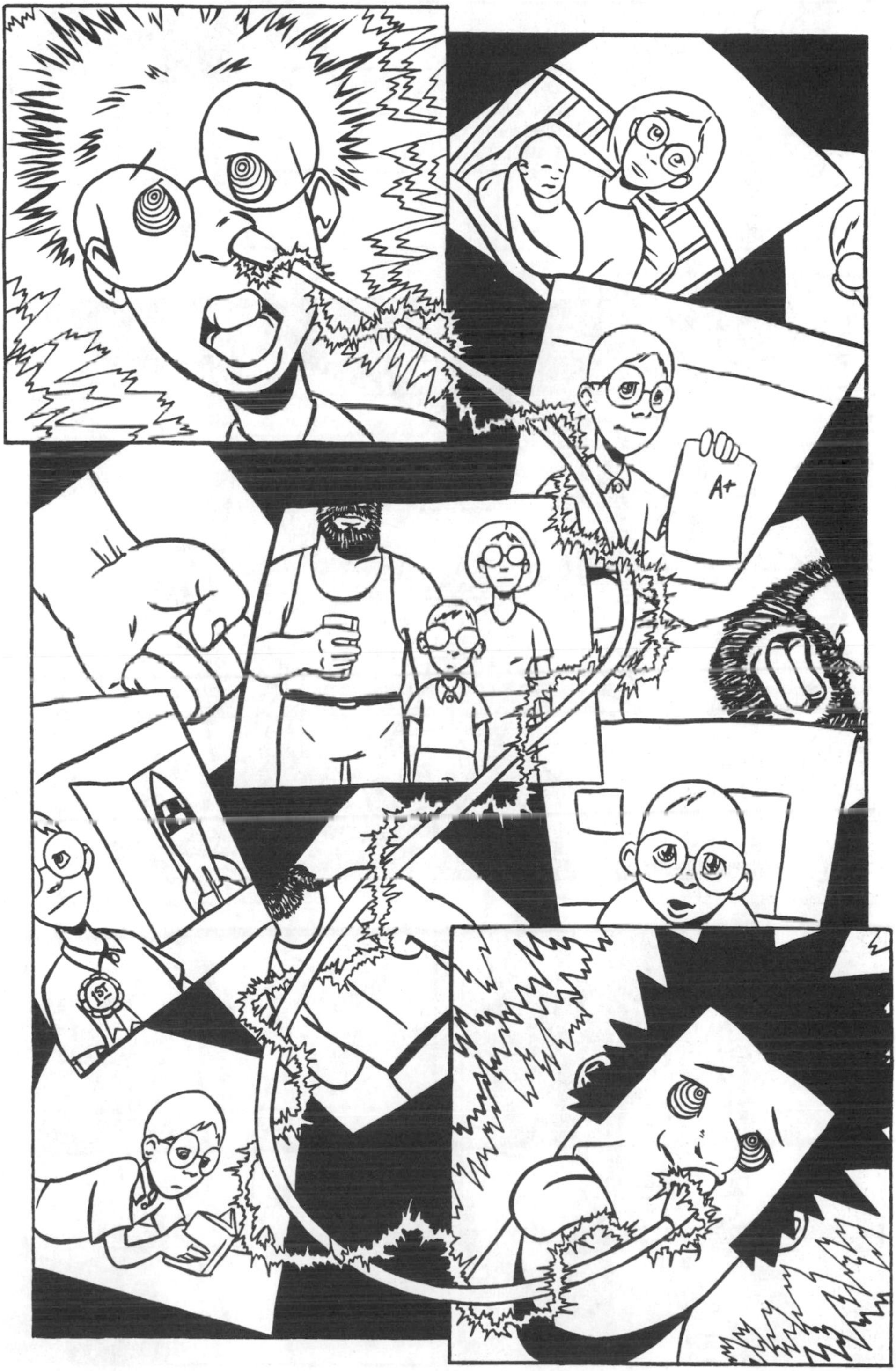
A+
1ST

OH DEAR. I MISTAKENLY DOWNLOADED THE I.D.S.P.'S MEMORIES INTO YOUR BRAIN, FRIEND. I APOLOGIZE PROFUSELY!

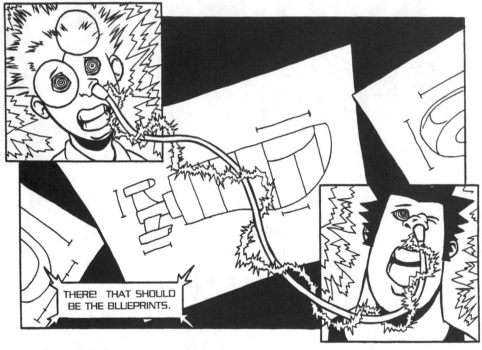

THERE! THAT SHOULD BE THE BLUEPRINTS.

SLAM

28

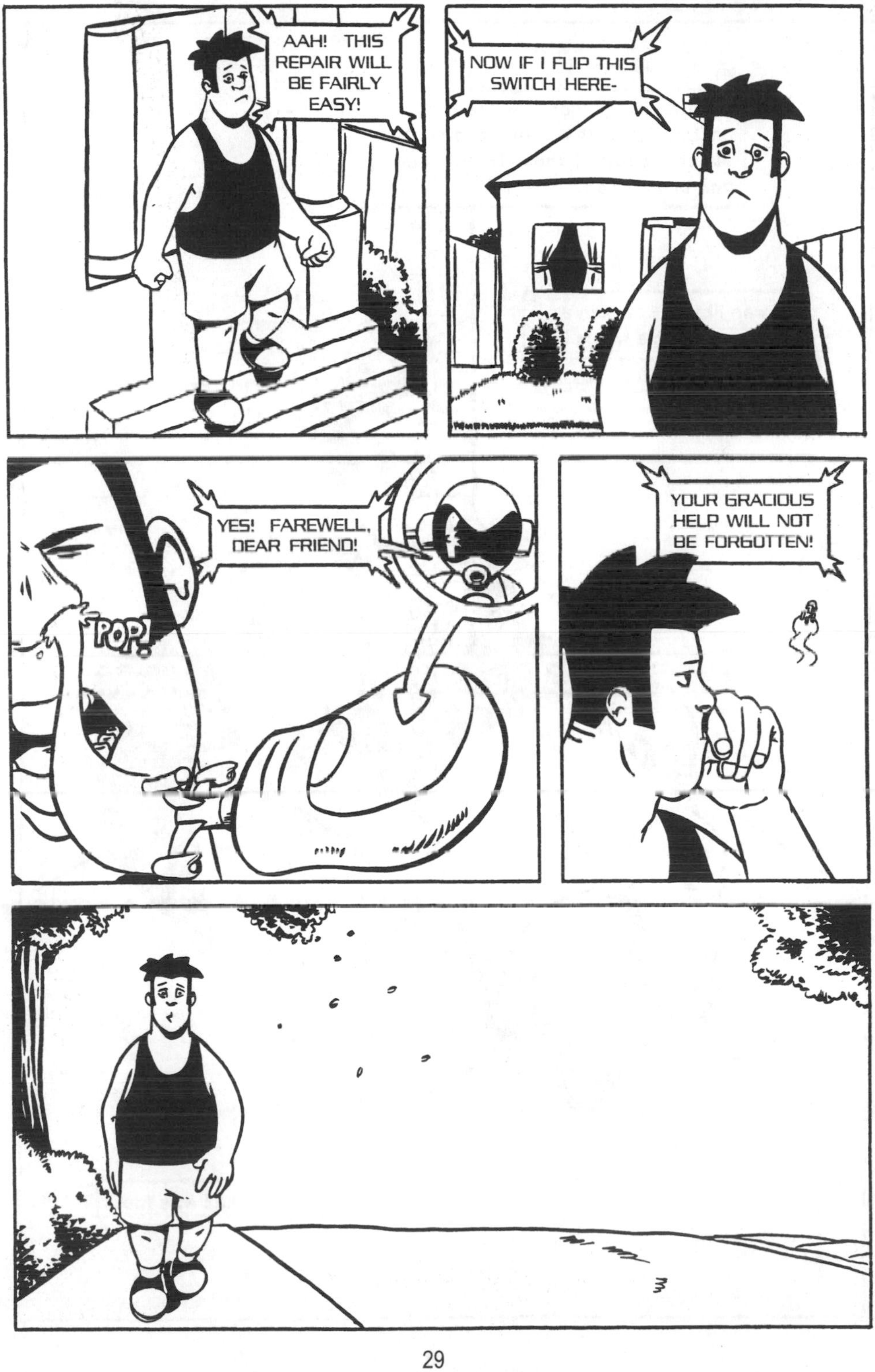
AAH! THIS REPAIR WILL BE FAIRLY EASY!
NOW IF I FLIP THIS SWITCH HERE-
YES! FAREWELL, DEAR FRIEND!
POP!
YOUR GRACIOUS HELP WILL NOT BE FORGOTTEN!

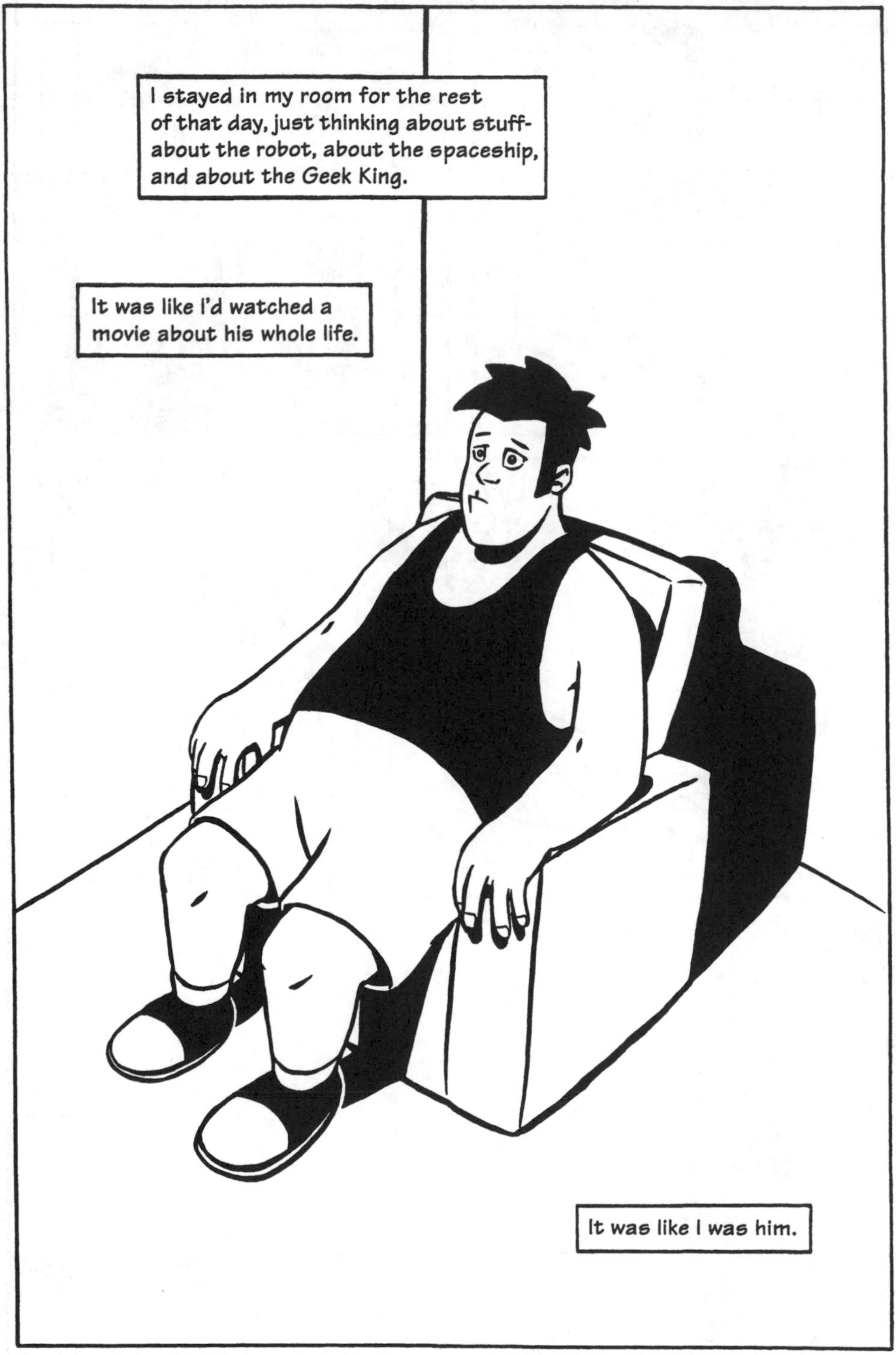
I stayed in my room for the rest of that day, just thinking about stuff- about the robot, about the spaceship, and about the Geek King.
It was like I'd watched a movie about his whole life.
It was like I was him.

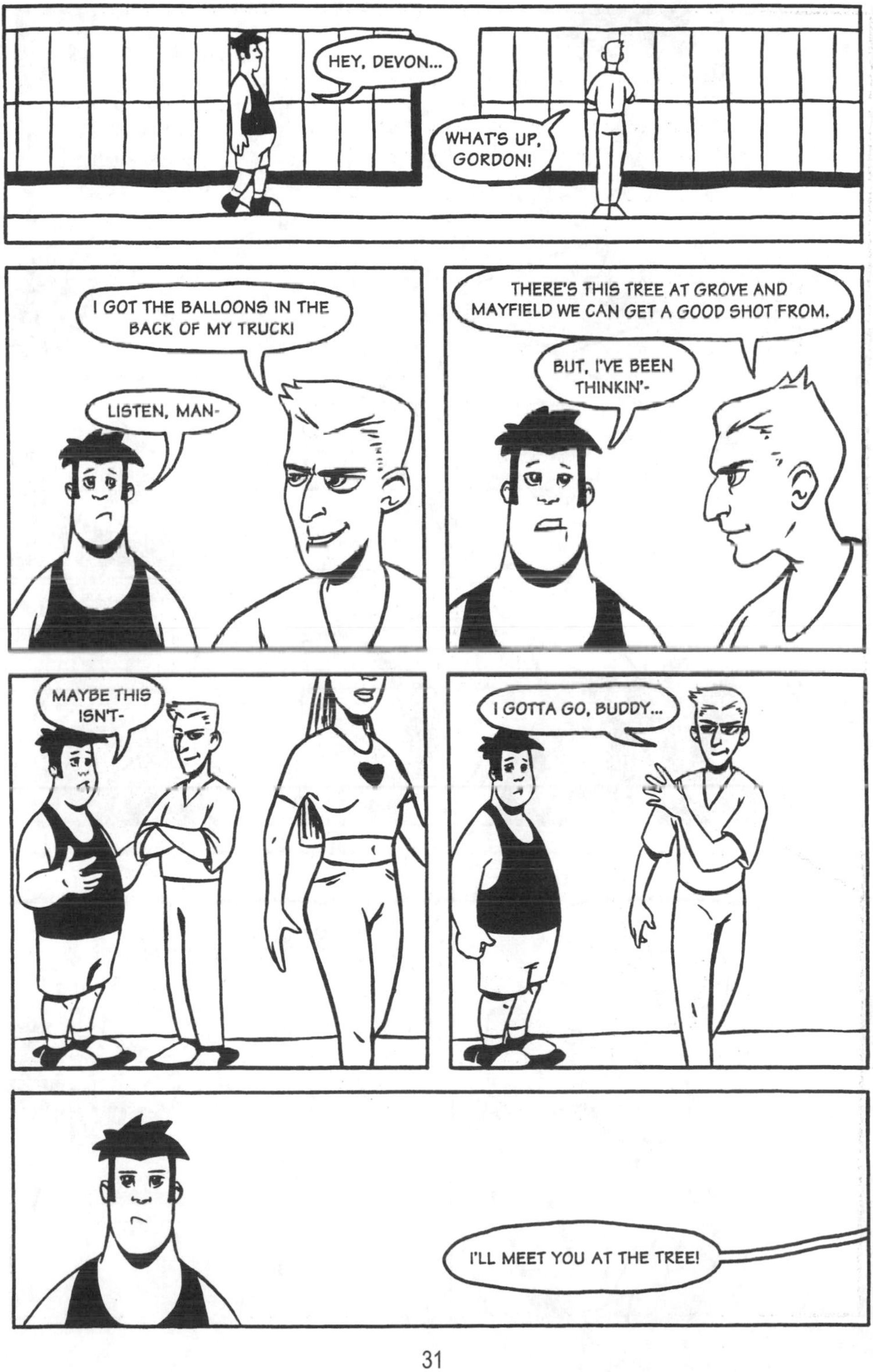
HEY, DEVON...
WHAT'S UP, GORDON!
I GOT THE BALLOONS IN THE BACK OF MY TRUCK!
LISTEN, MAN-
THERE'S THIS TREE AT GROVE AND MAYFIELD WE CAN GET A GOOD SHOT FROM.
BUT, I'VE BEEN THINKIN'-
MAYBE THIS ISN'T-
I GOTTA GO, BUDDY...
I'LL MEET YOU AT THE TREE!

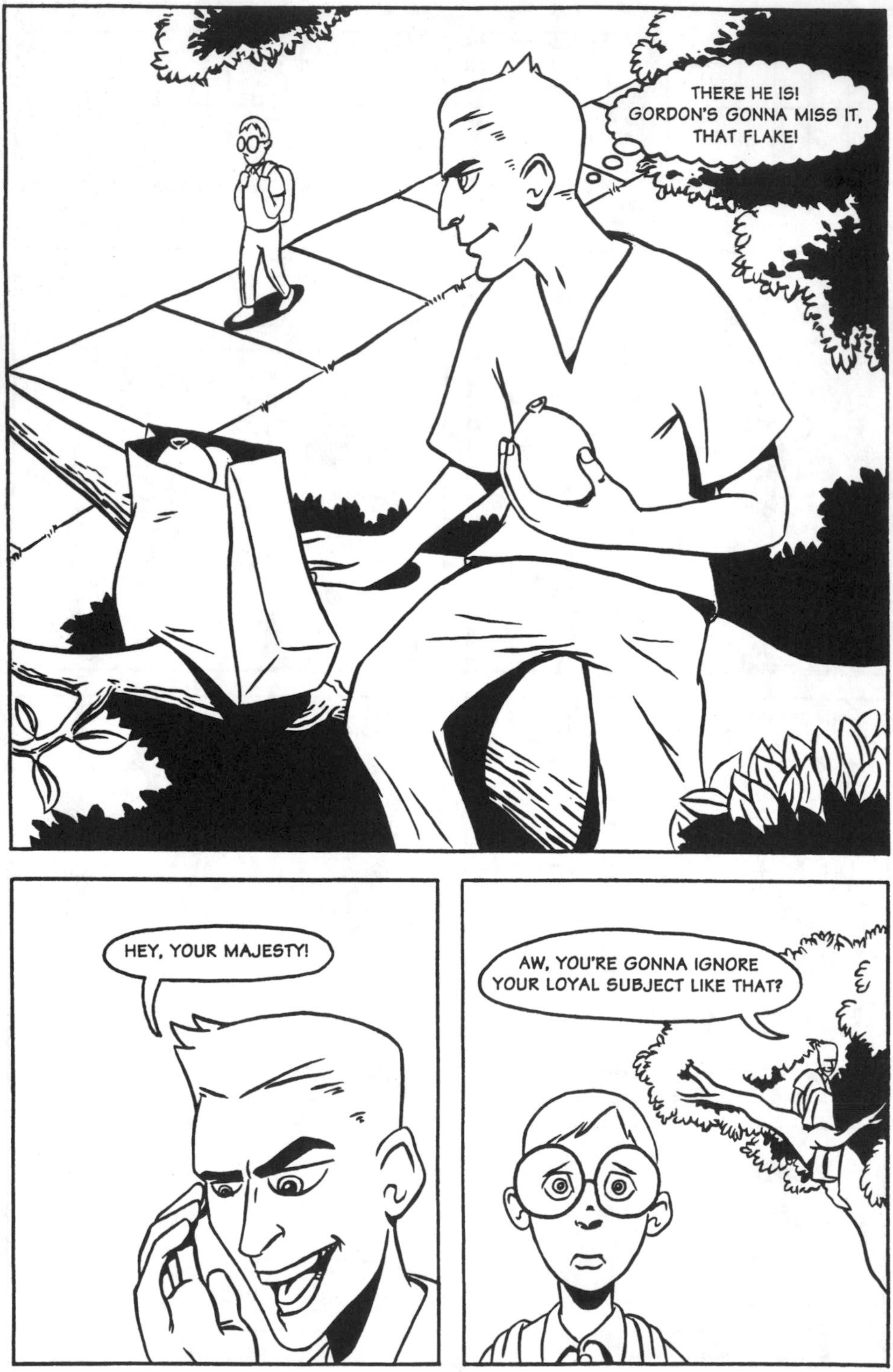
THERE HE IS! GORDON'S GONNA MISS IT, THAT FLAKE!
HEY, YOUR MAJESTY!
AW, YOU'RE GONNA IGNORE YOUR LOYAL SUBJECT LIKE THAT?

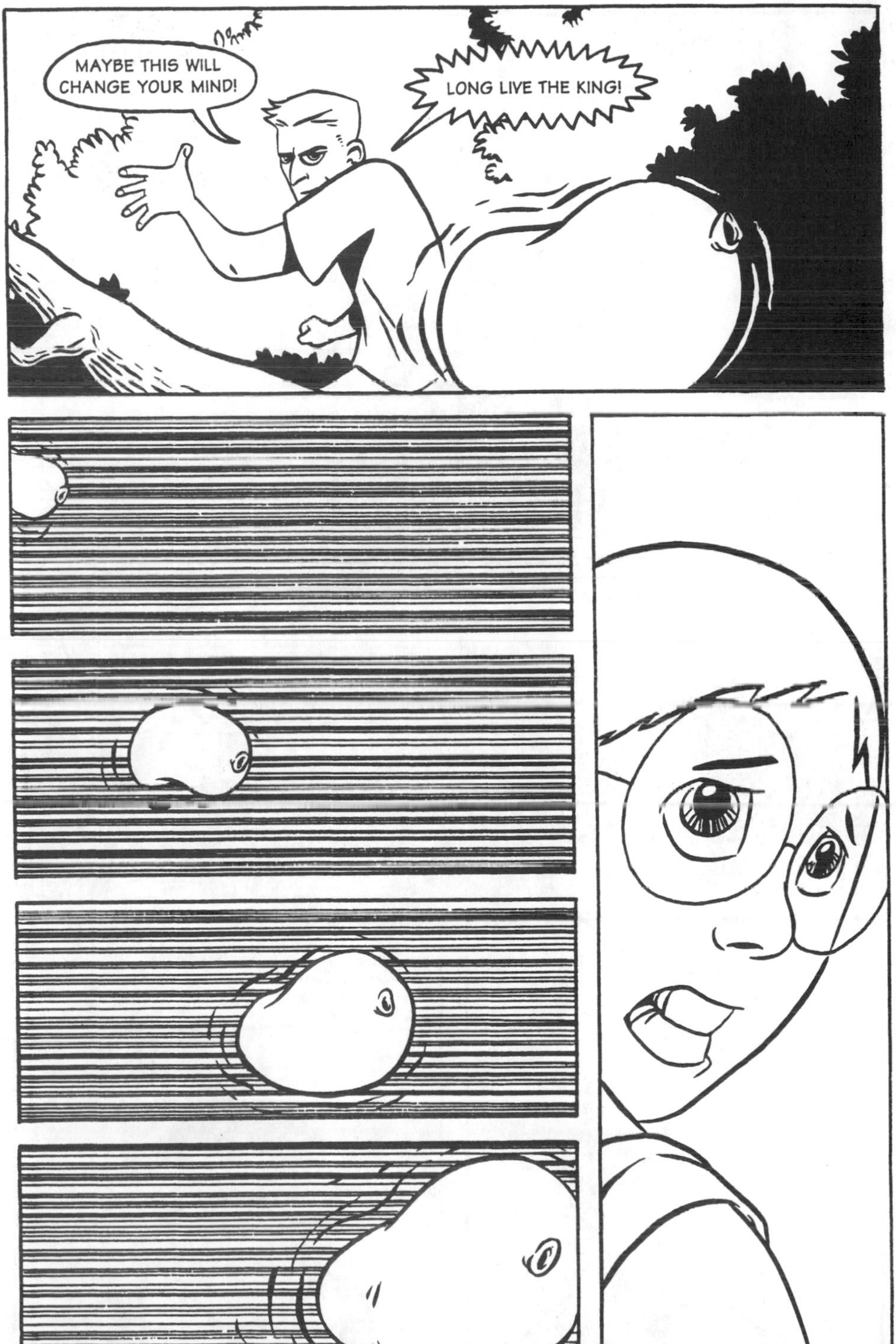
MAYBE THIS WILL CHANGE YOUR MIND!
LONG LIVE THE KING!

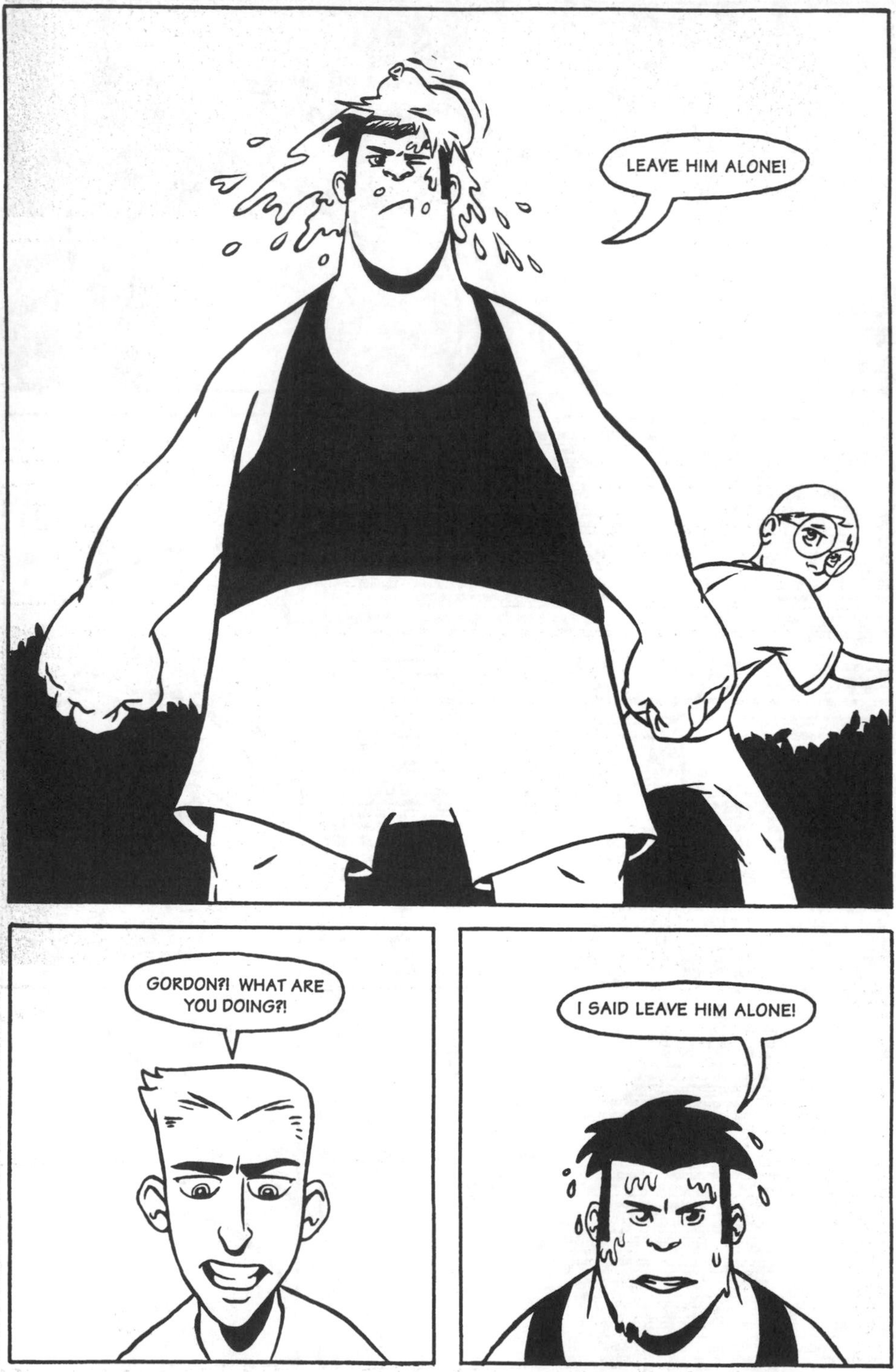
LEAVE HIM ALONE!
GORDON?! WHAT ARE YOU DOING?!
I SAID LEAVE HIM ALONE!

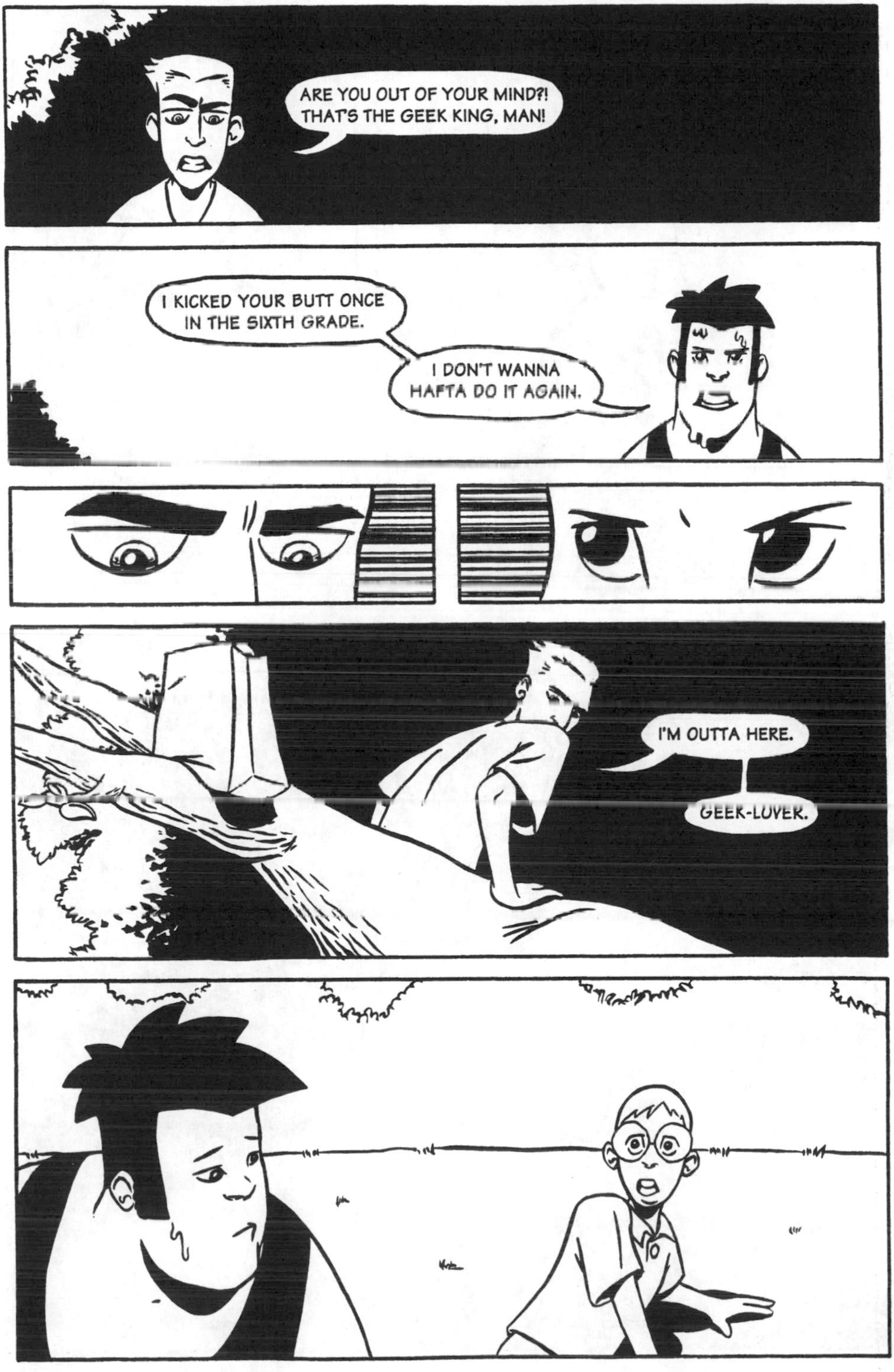
ARE YOU OUT OF YOUR MIND?! THAT'S THE GEEK KING, MAN!
I KICKED YOUR BUTT ONCE IN THE SIXTH GRADE.
I DON'T WANNA HAFTA DO IT AGAIN.
I'M OUTTA HERE.
GEEK-LOVER.

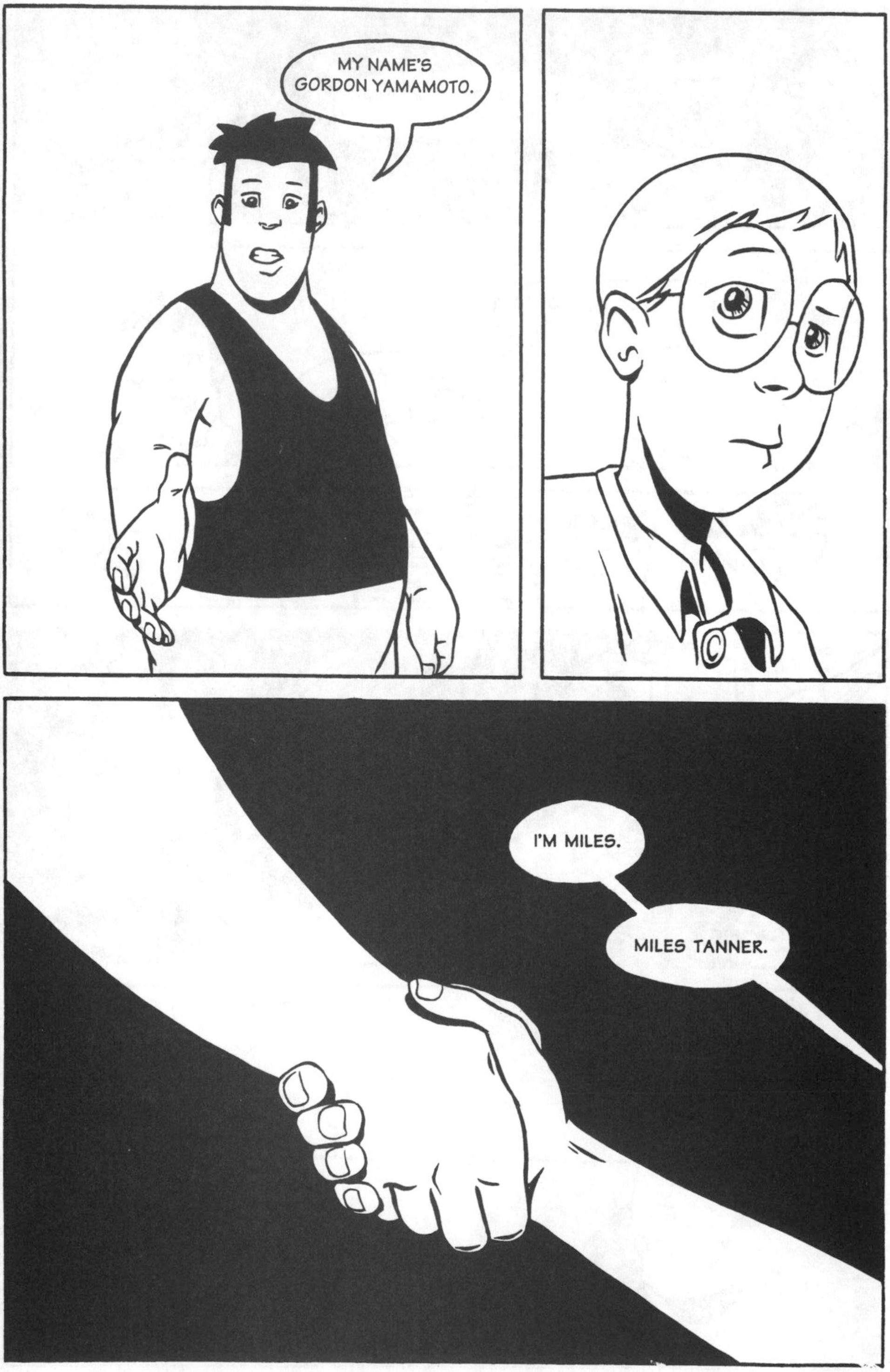
MY NAME'S
GORDON YAMAMOTO.
I'M MILES.
MILES TANNER.

CHAPTER TWO

2

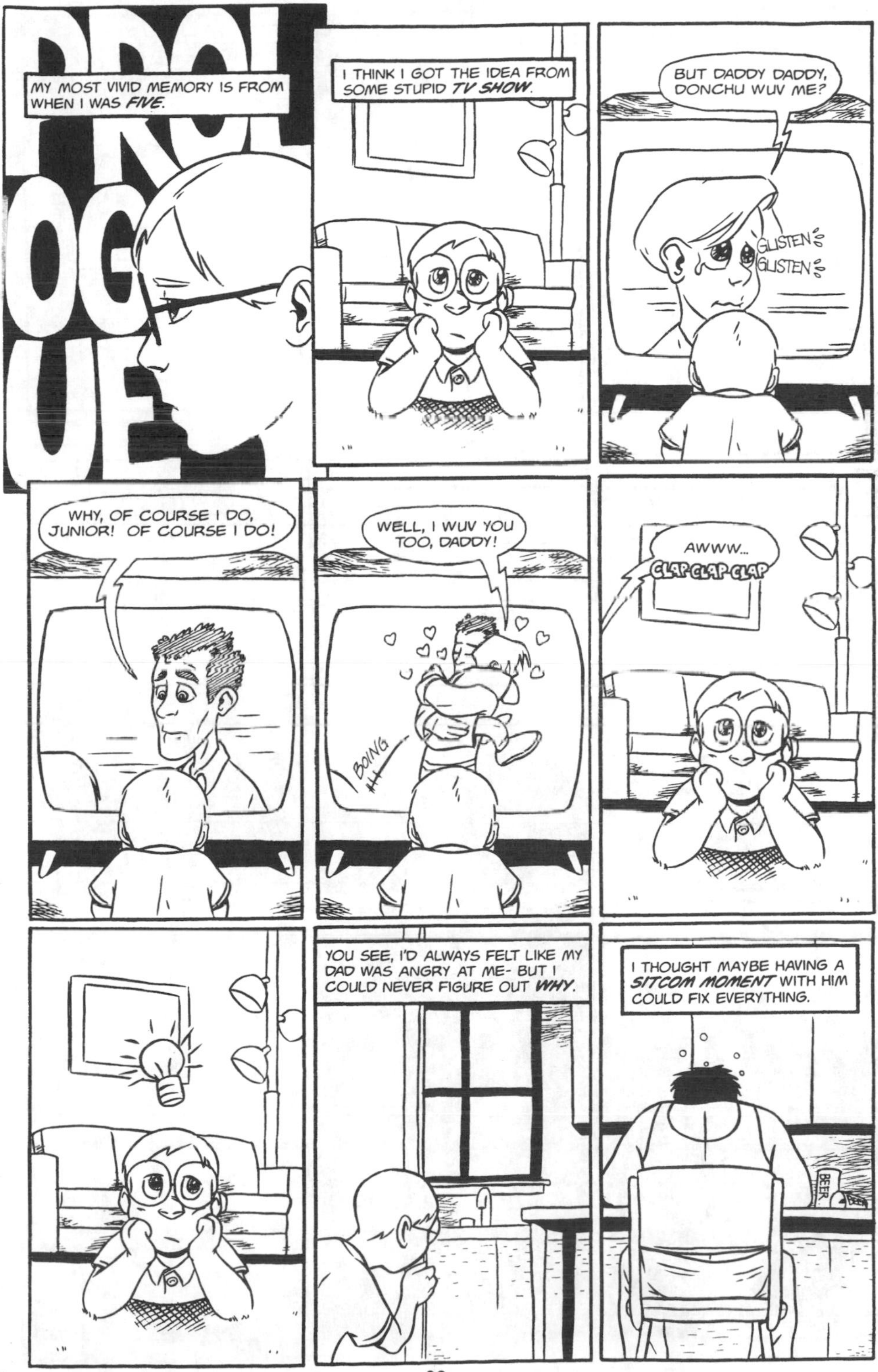
PROLOGUE
MY MOST VIVID MEMORY IS FROM WHEN I WAS *FIVE*.
I THINK I GOT THE IDEA FROM SOME STUPID *TV SHOW*.
BUT DADDY DADDY, DONCHU WUV ME?
GLISTEN
GLISTEN
WHY, OF COURSE I DO, JUNIOR! OF COURSE I DO!
WELL, I WUV YOU TOO, DADDY!
BOING
AWWW...
CLAP CLAP CLAP
YOU SEE, I'D ALWAYS FELT LIKE MY DAD WAS ANGRY AT ME- BUT I COULD NEVER FIGURE OUT *WHY*.
I THOUGHT MAYBE HAVING A *SITCOM MOMENT* WITH HIM COULD FIX EVERYTHING.
BEER

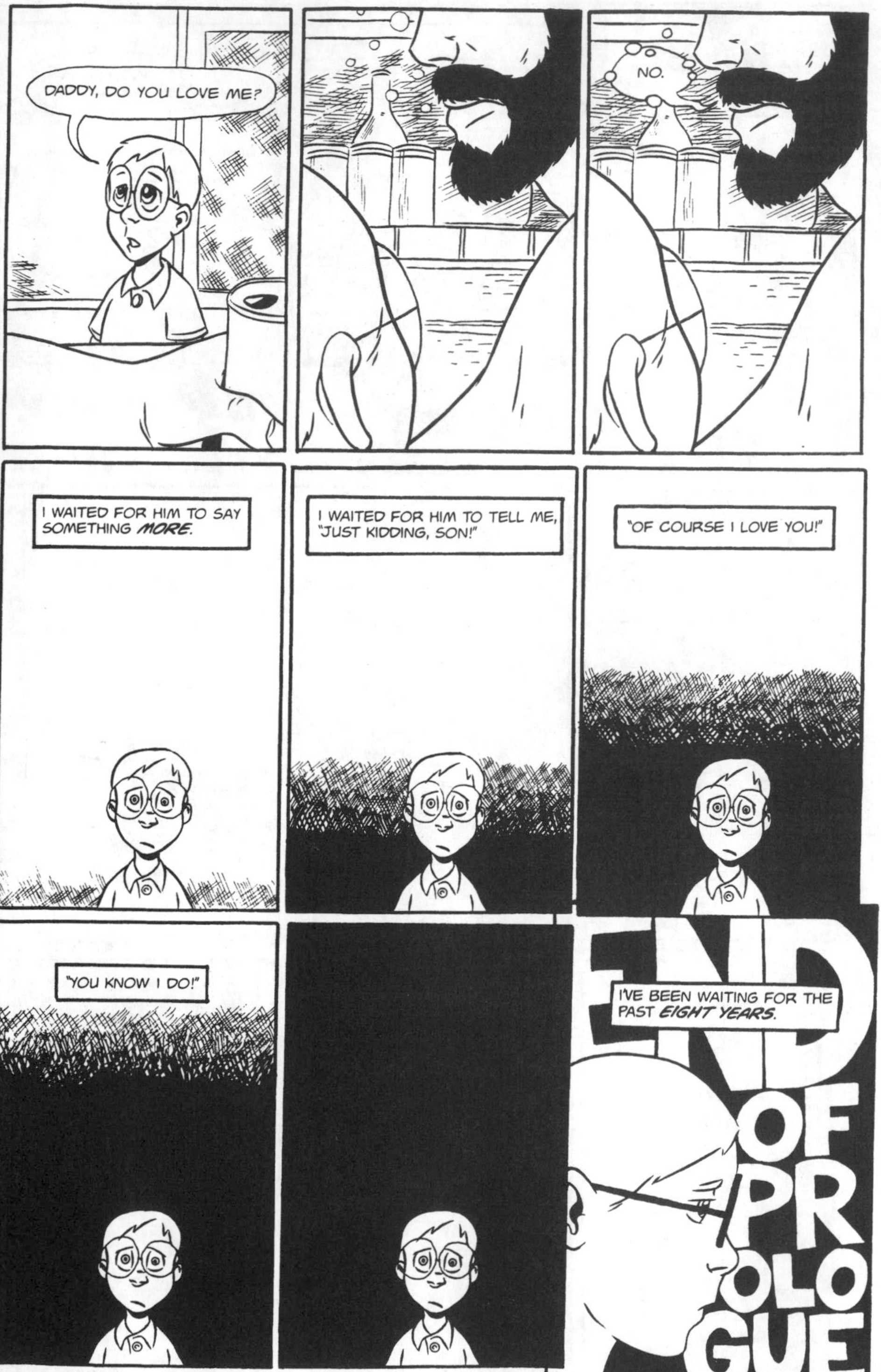
DADDY, DO YOU LOVE ME?
NO.
I WAITED FOR HIM TO SAY SOMETHING *MORE*.
I WAITED FOR HIM TO TELL ME, "JUST KIDDING, SON!"
"OF COURSE I LOVE YOU!"
"YOU KNOW I DO!"
I'VE BEEN WAITING FOR THE PAST *EIGHT YEARS*.
END OF PROLOGUE

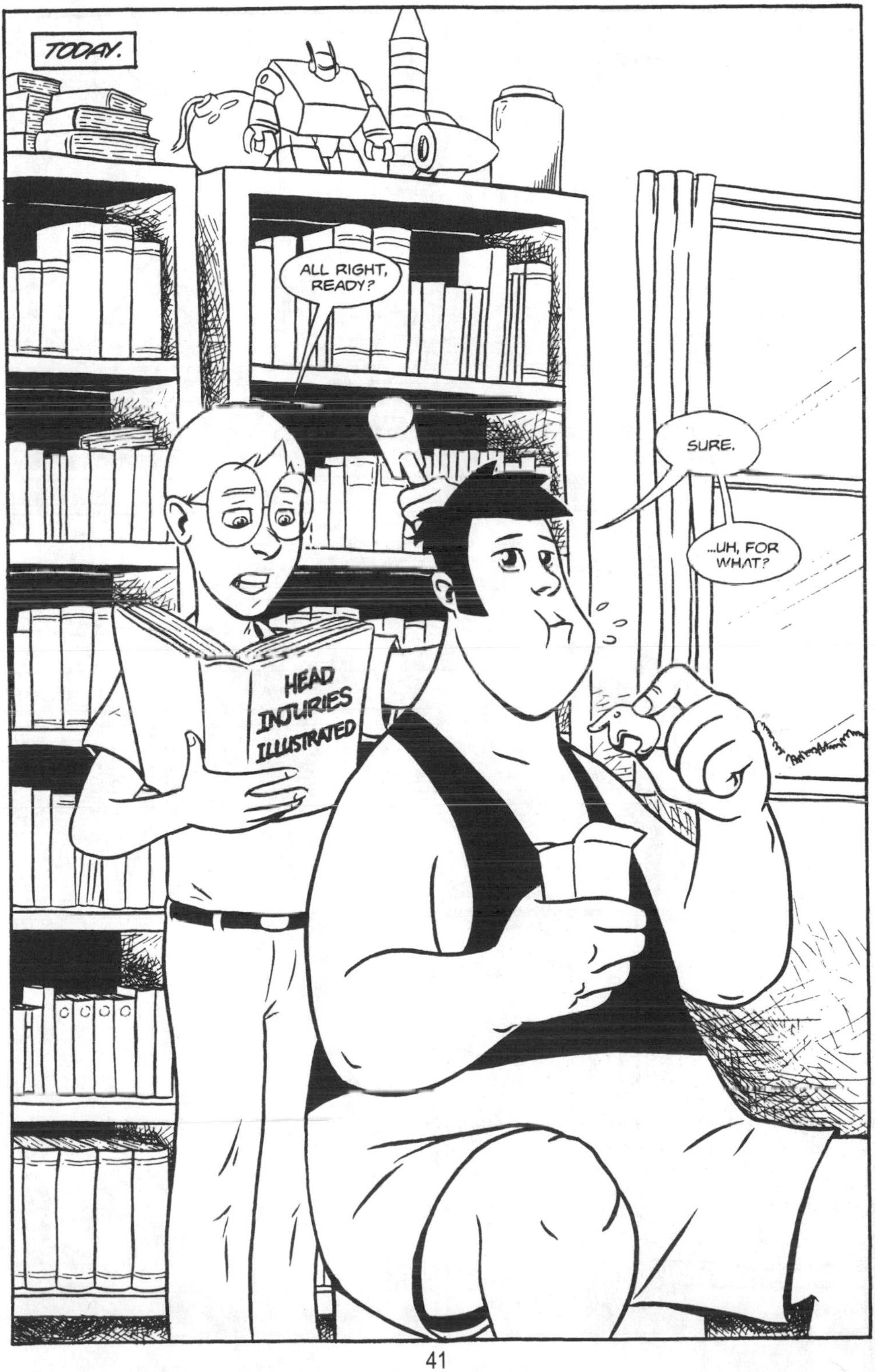
TODAY.
ALL RIGHT, READY?
SURE.
...UH, FOR WHAT?
HEAD INJURIES ILLUSTRATED

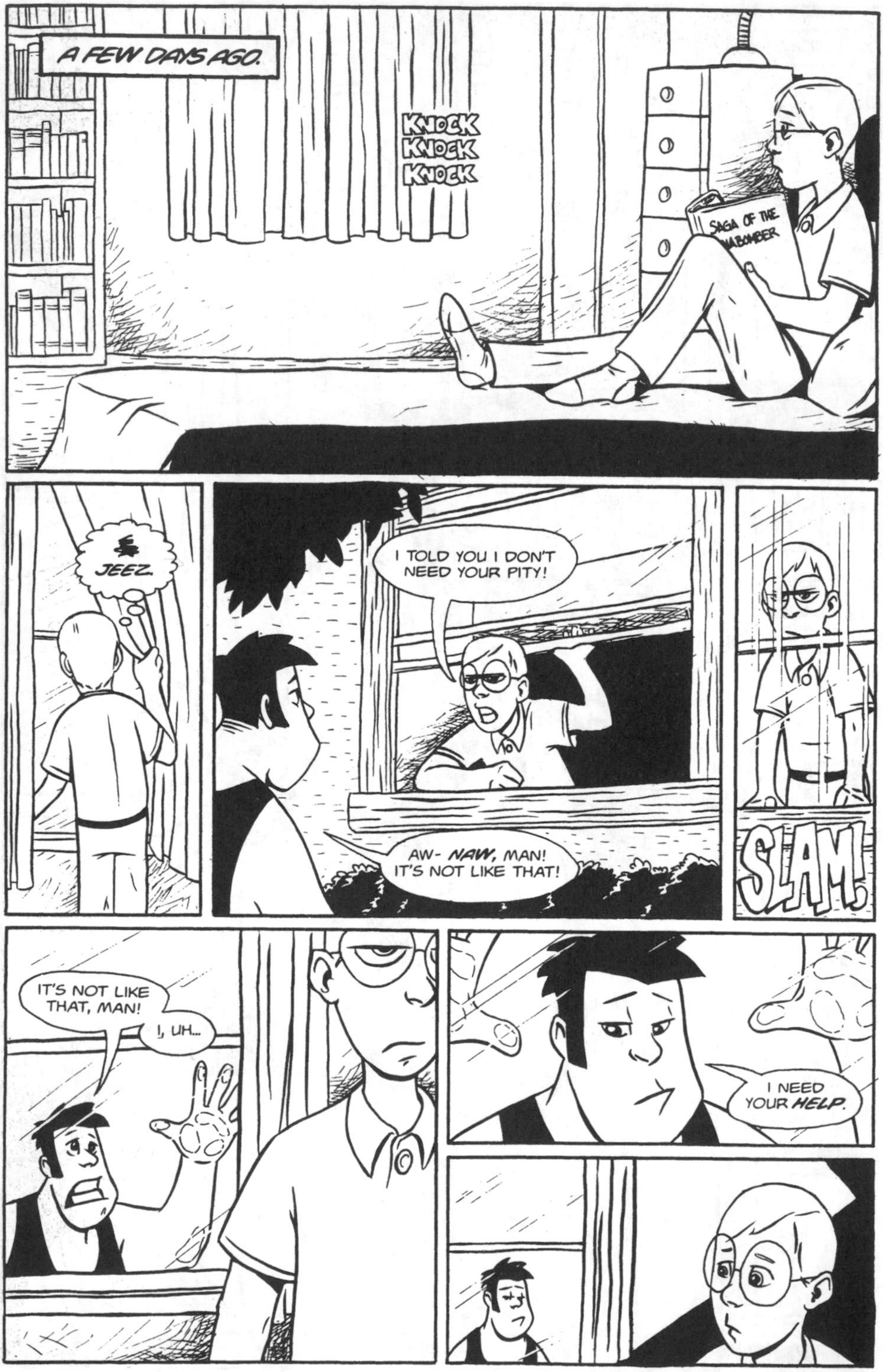
A FEW DAYS AGO.
KNOCK
KNOCK
KNOCK
SAGA OF THE UNABOMBER
JEEZ.
I TOLD YOU I DON'T NEED YOUR PITY!
AW- NAW, MAN! IT'S NOT LIKE THAT!
SLAM!
IT'S NOT LIKE THAT, MAN!
I, UH...
I NEED YOUR HELP.

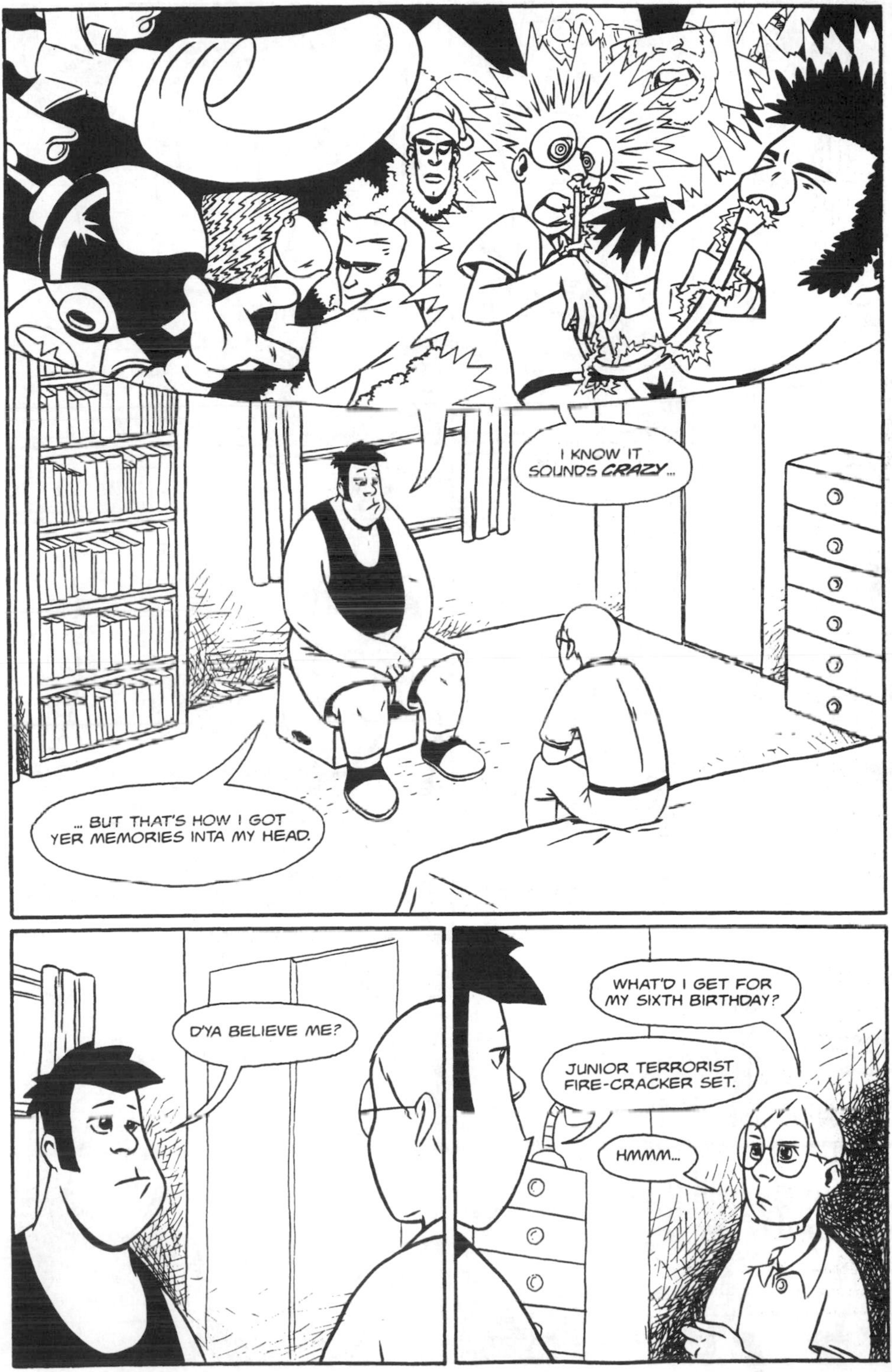
I KNOW IT SOUNDS CRAZY...
... BUT THAT'S HOW I GOT YER MEMORIES INTA MY HEAD.
D'YA BELIEVE ME?
WHAT'D I GET FOR MY SIXTH BIRTHDAY?
JUNIOR TERRORIST FIRE-CRACKER SET.
HMMM...

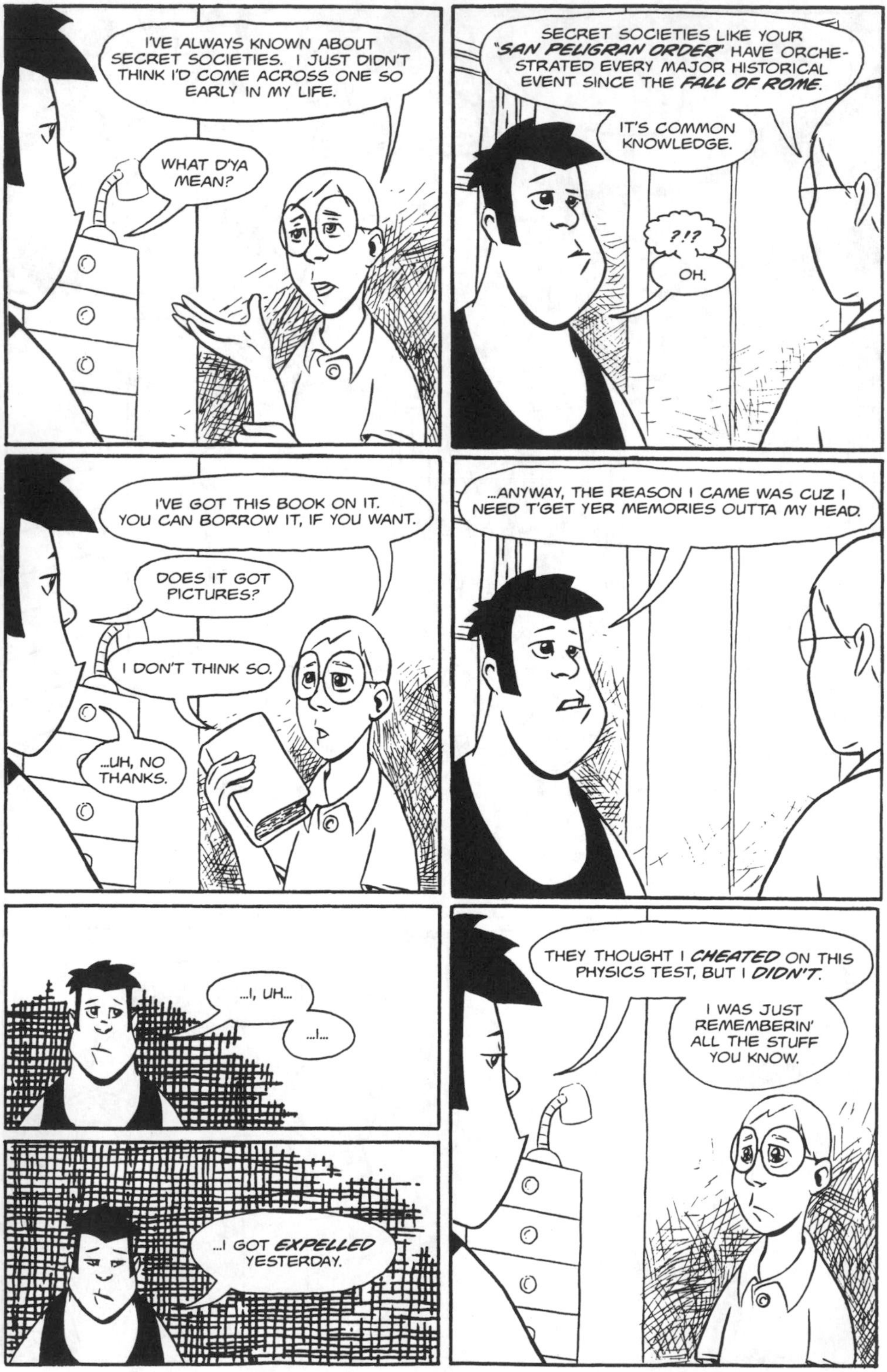
I'VE ALWAYS KNOWN ABOUT SECRET SOCIETIES. I JUST DIDN'T THINK I'D COME ACROSS ONE SO EARLY IN MY LIFE.
WHAT D'YA MEAN?
SECRET SOCIETIES LIKE YOUR "SAN PELIGRAN ORDER" HAVE ORCHESTRATED EVERY MAJOR HISTORICAL EVENT SINCE THE FALL OF ROME.
IT'S COMMON KNOWLEDGE.
?!?
OH.
I'VE GOT THIS BOOK ON IT. YOU CAN BORROW IT, IF YOU WANT.
DOES IT GOT PICTURES?
I DON'T THINK SO.
...UH, NO THANKS.
...ANYWAY, THE REASON I CAME WAS CUZ I NEED T'GET YER MEMORIES OUTTA MY HEAD.
...I, UH...
...I...
...I GOT EXPELLED YESTERDAY.
THEY THOUGHT I CHEATED ON THIS PHYSICS TEST, BUT I DIDN'T.
I WAS JUST REMEMBERIN' ALL THE STUFF YOU KNOW.

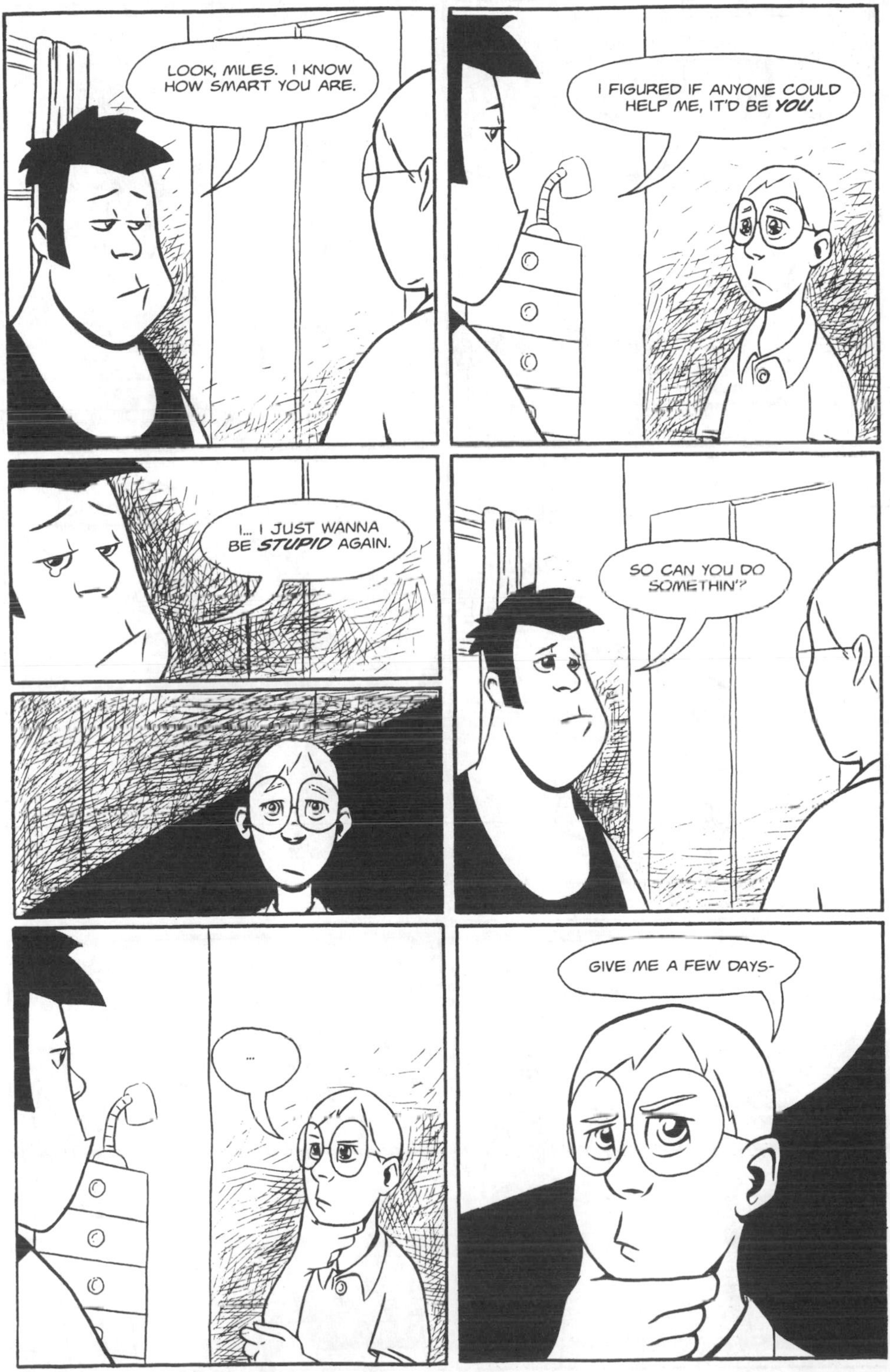
LOOK, MILES. I KNOW HOW SMART YOU ARE.
I FIGURED IF ANYONE COULD HELP ME, IT'D BE *YOU*.
I... I JUST WANNA BE ***STUPID*** AGAIN.
SO CAN YOU DO SOMETHIN'?
...
GIVE ME A FEW DAYS-

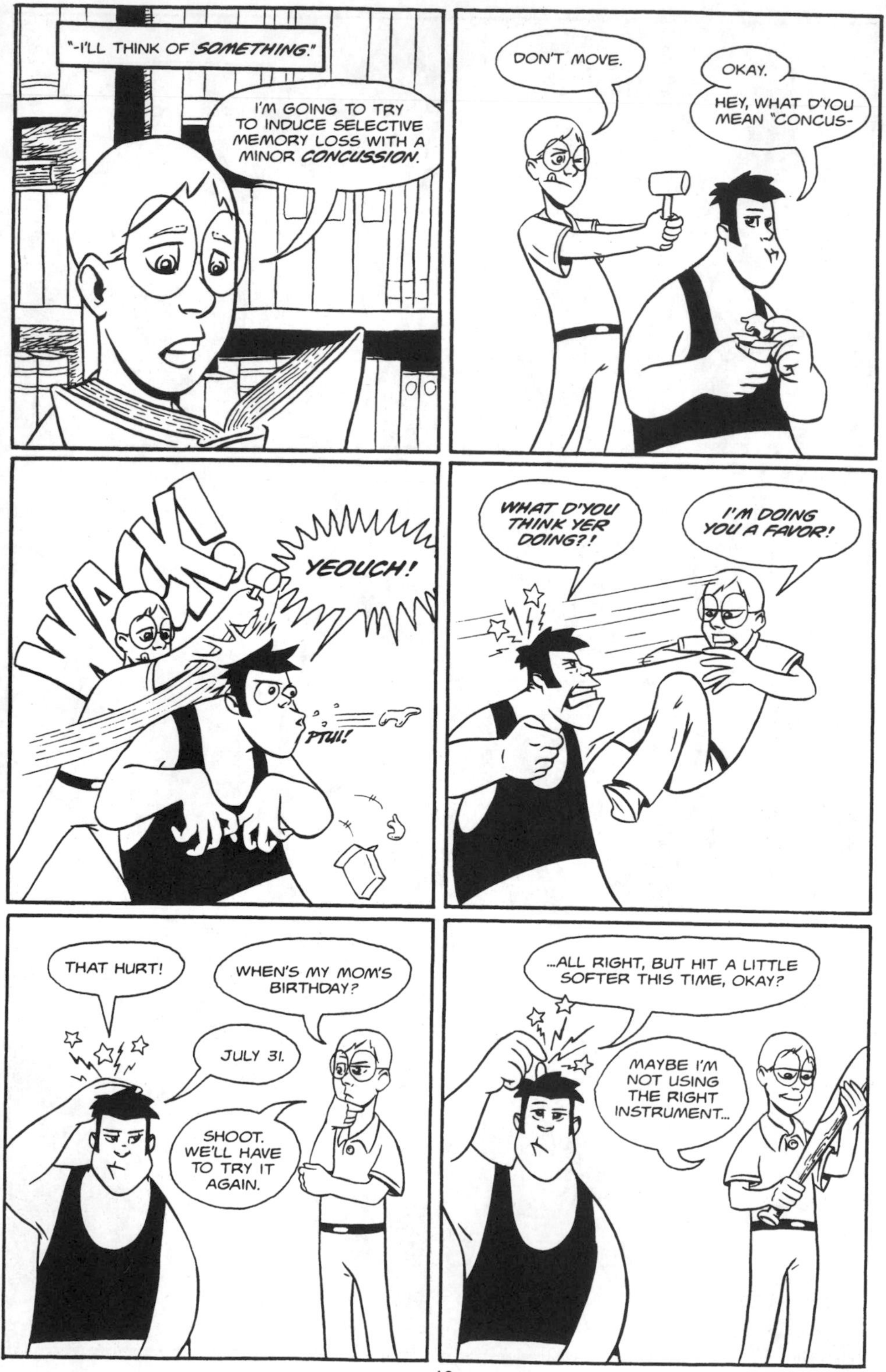
"-I'LL THINK OF *SOMETHING*."
I'M GOING TO TRY TO INDUCE SELECTIVE MEMORY LOSS WITH A MINOR *CONCUSSION*.
DON'T MOVE.
OKAY.
HEY, WHAT D'YOU MEAN "CONCUS-
WACK!
YEOUCH!
PTUI!
WHAT D'YOU THINK YER DOING?!
I'M DOING YOU A FAVOR!
THAT HURT!
WHEN'S MY MOM'S BIRTHDAY?
JULY 31.
SHOOT. WE'LL HAVE TO TRY IT AGAIN.
...ALL RIGHT, BUT HIT A LITTLE SOFTER THIS TIME, OKAY?
MAYBE I'M NOT USING THE RIGHT INSTRUMENT...

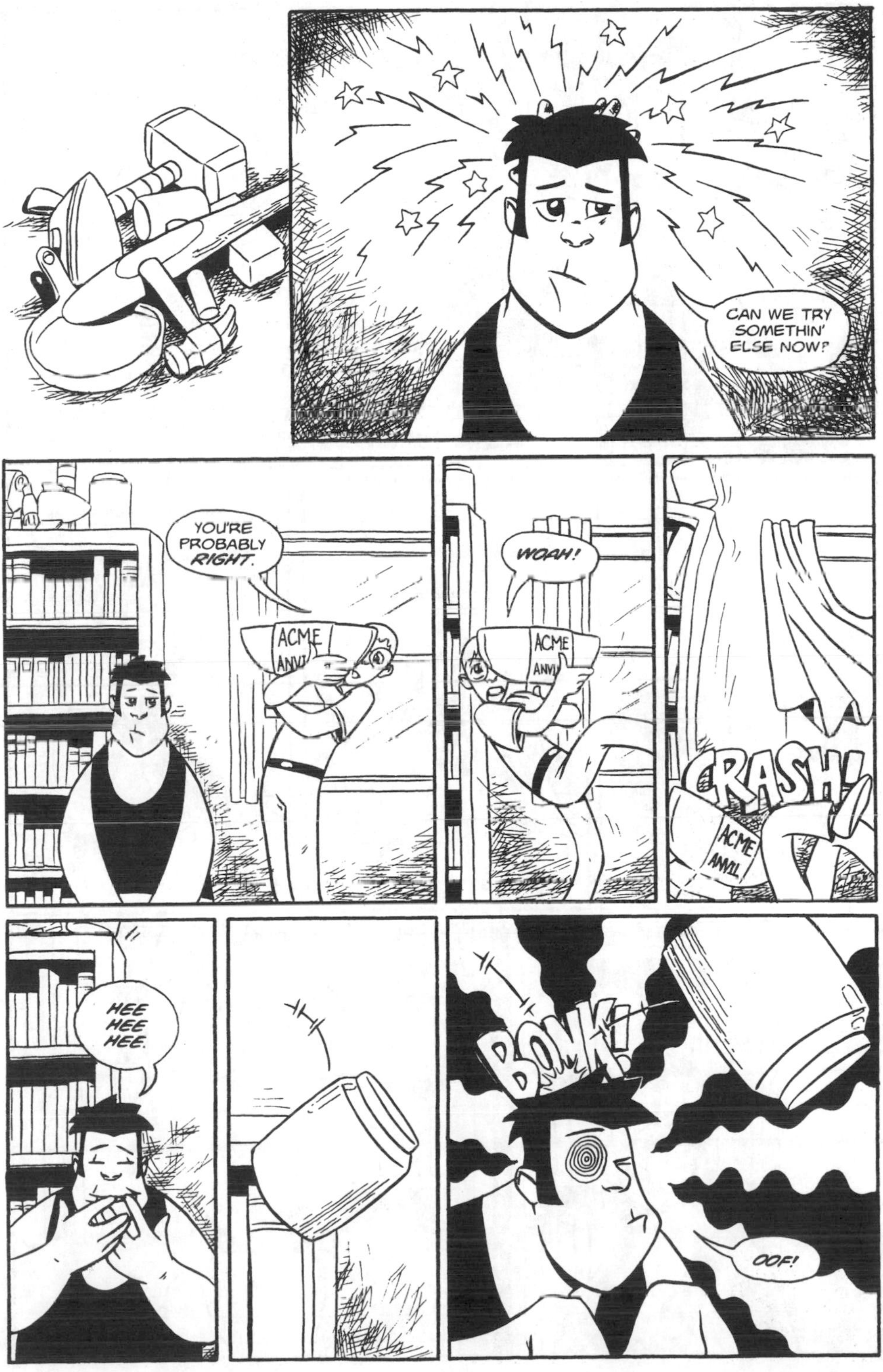
CAN WE TRY SOMETHIN' ELSE NOW?
YOU'RE PROBABLY RIGHT.
ACME ANVIL
WOAH!
ACME ANVIL
CRASH!
ACME ANVIL
HEE HEE HEE.
BONK!
OOF!

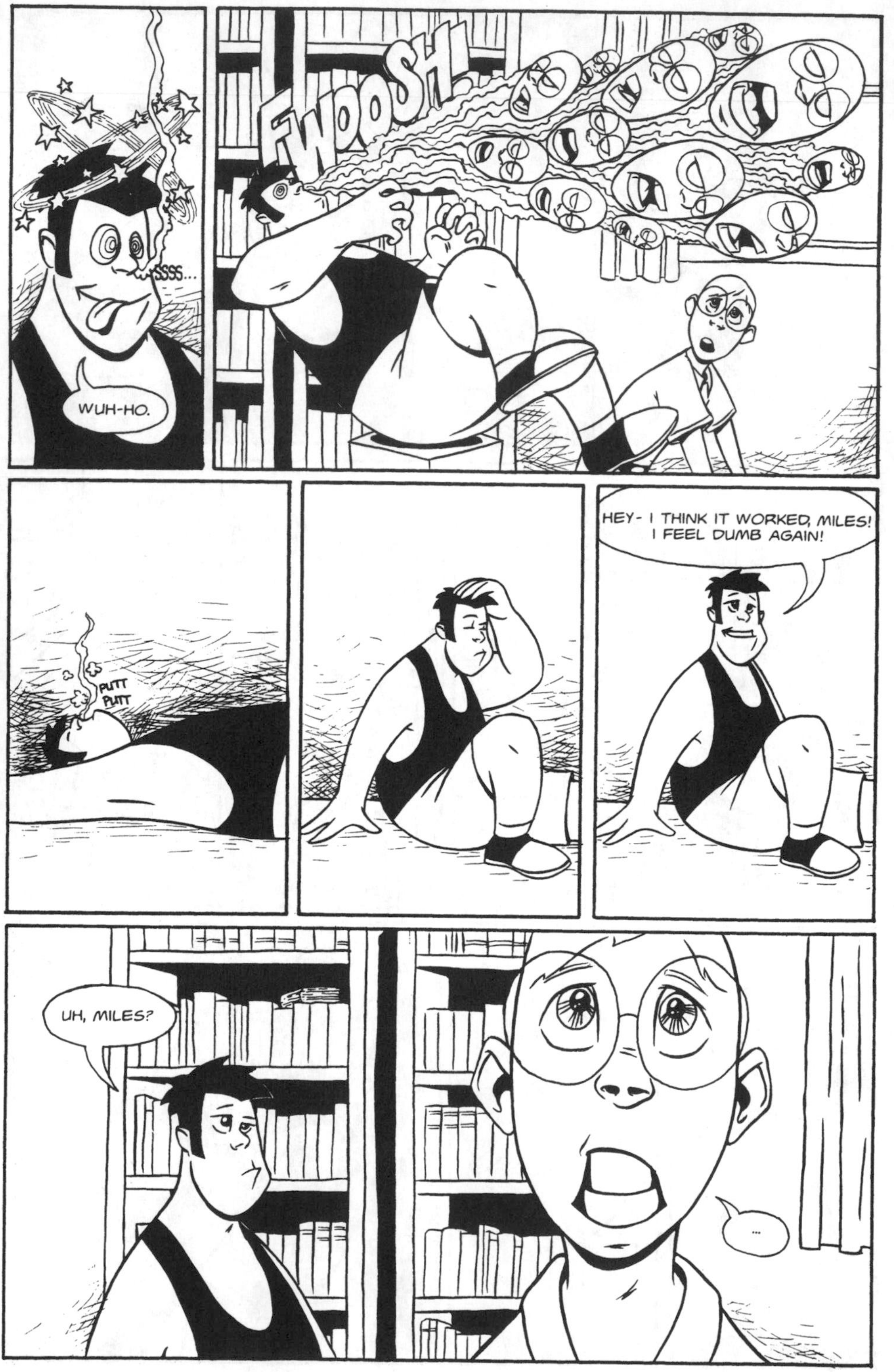

SSSS...
WUH-HO.
FWOOSH!
PUTT PUTT
HEY- I THINK IT WORKED, MILES! I FEEL DUMB AGAIN!
UH, MILES?
...

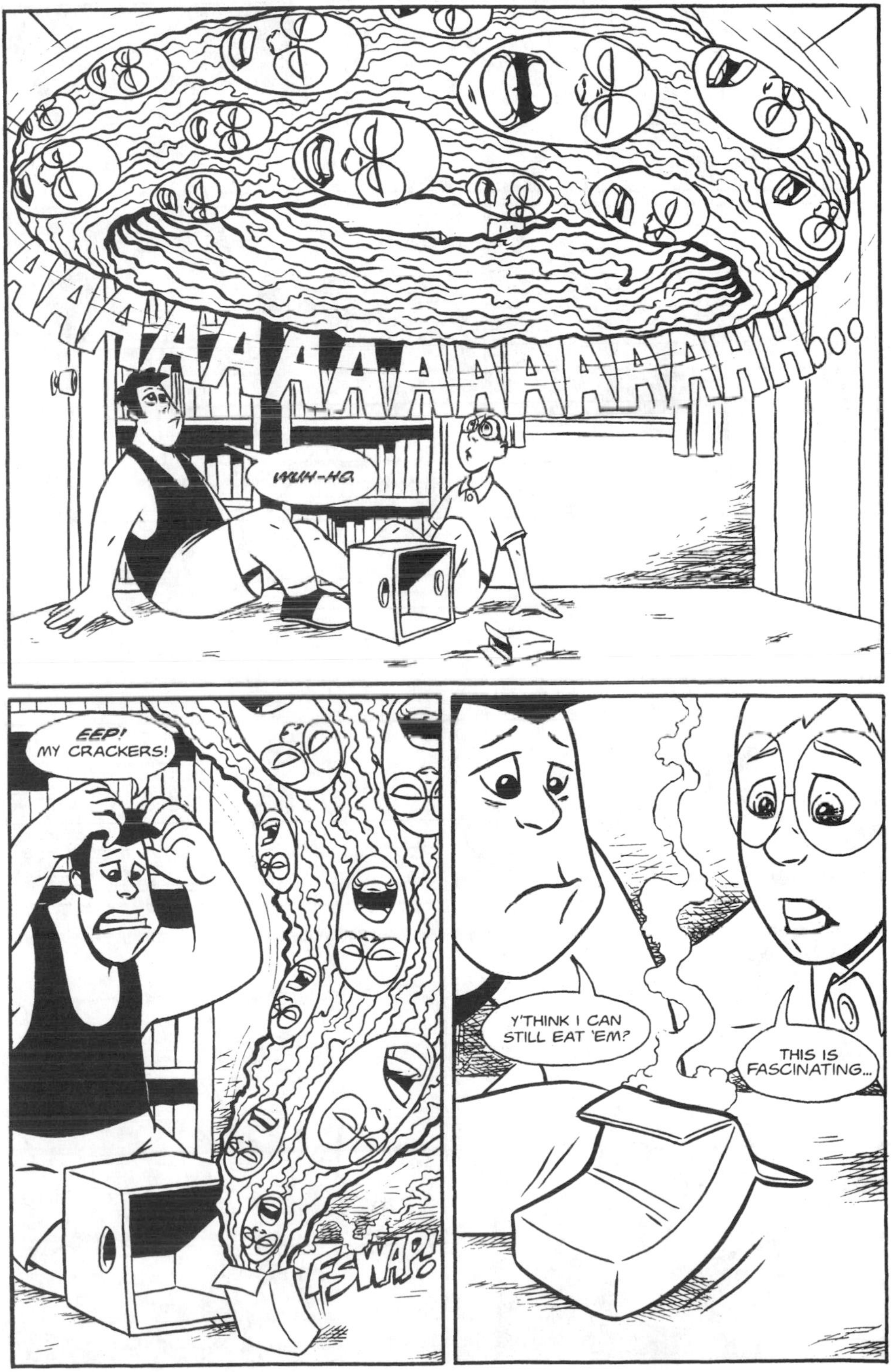
AAAAAAAAAAAAAAAAAHH...
WUH-HO.
EEP! MY CRACKERS!
FSWAP!
Y'THINK I CAN STILL EAT 'EM?
THIS IS FASCINATING...

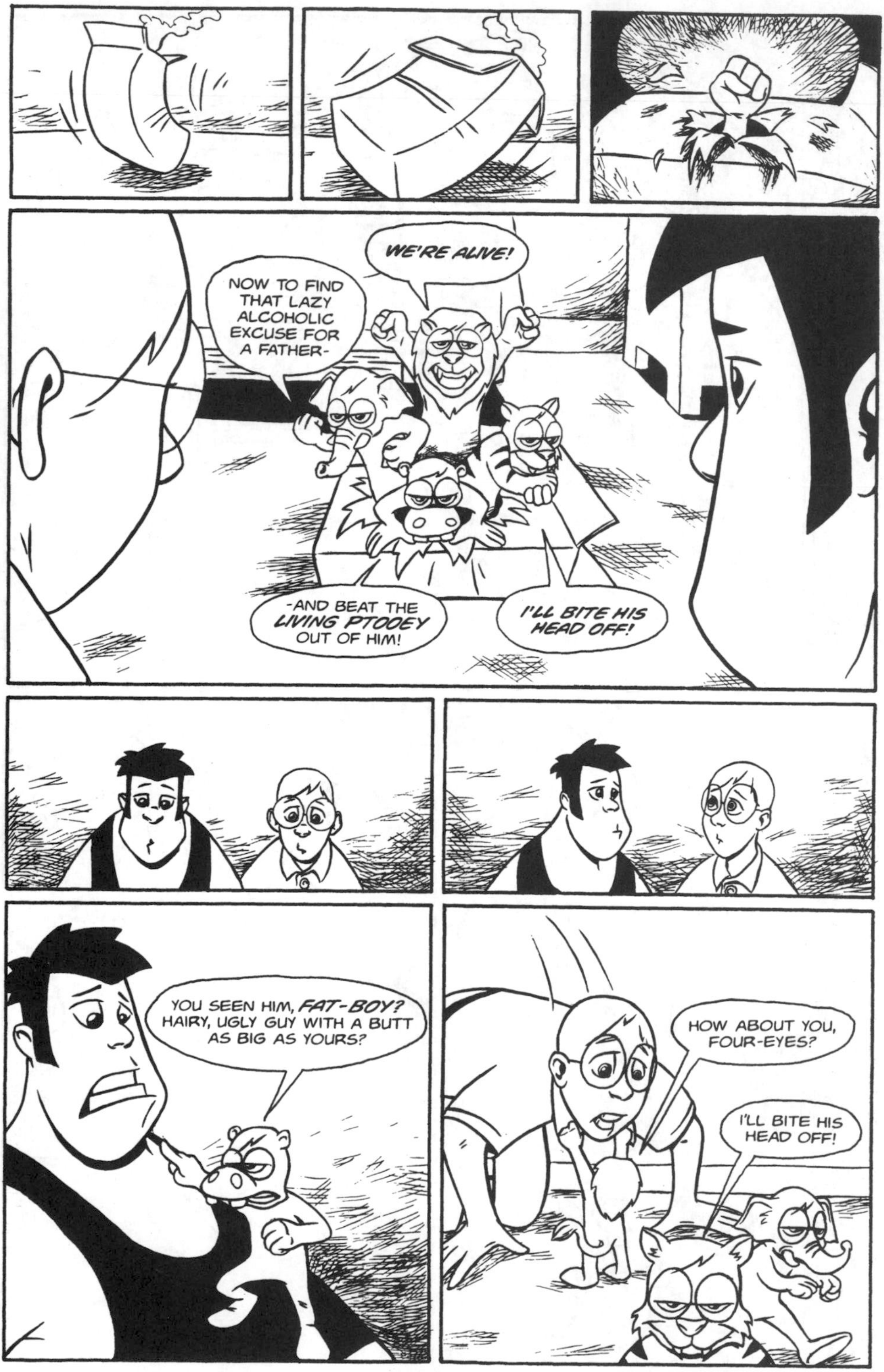
NOW TO FIND THAT LAZY ALCOHOLIC EXCUSE FOR A FATHER-
WE'RE ALIVE!
-AND BEAT THE LIVING PTOOEY OUT OF HIM!
I'LL BITE HIS HEAD OFF!
YOU SEEN HIM, FAT-BOY? HAIRY, UGLY GUY WITH A BUTT AS BIG AS YOURS?
HOW ABOUT YOU, FOUR-EYES?
I'LL BITE HIS HEAD OFF!

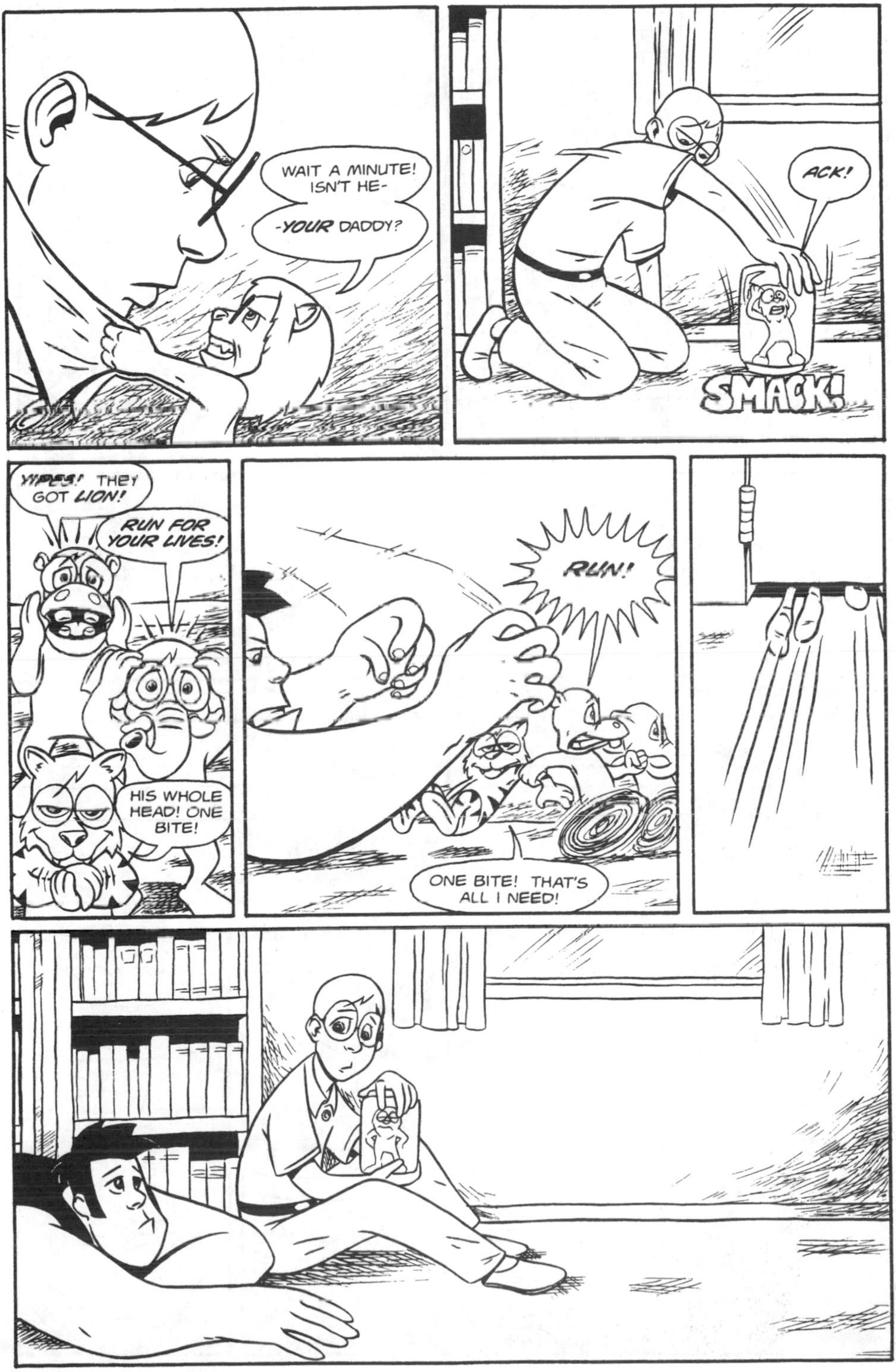
WAIT A MINUTE! ISN'T HE-
-YOUR DADDY?
ACK!
SMACK!
YIPES! THEY GOT LION!
RUN FOR YOUR LIVES!
HIS WHOLE HEAD! ONE BITE!
RUN!
ONE BITE! THAT'S ALL I NEED!

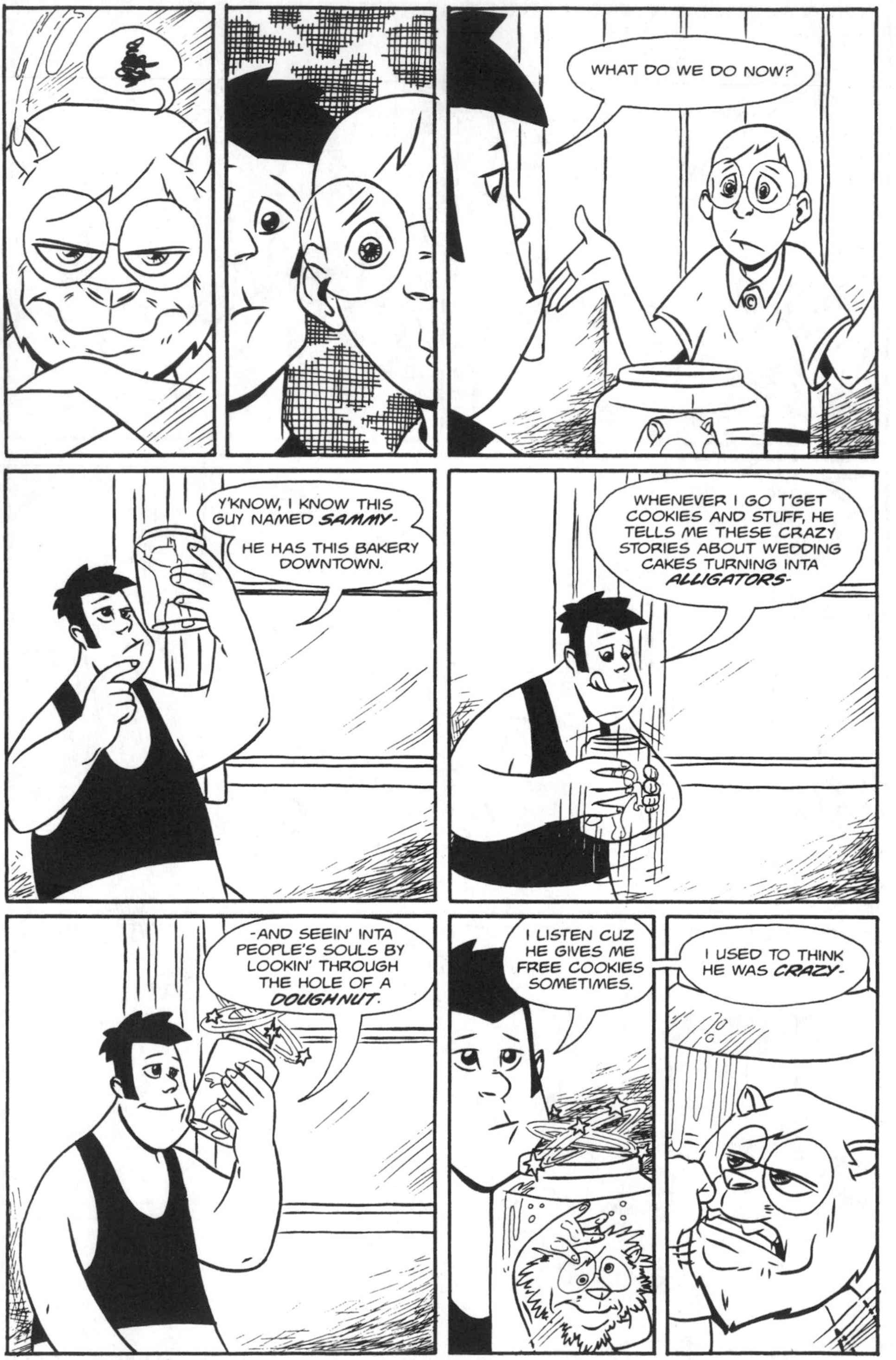
WHAT DO WE DO NOW?
Y'KNOW, I KNOW THIS GUY NAMED SAMMY-
HE HAS THIS BAKERY DOWNTOWN.
WHENEVER I GO T'GET COOKIES AND STUFF, HE TELLS ME THESE CRAZY STORIES ABOUT WEDDING CAKES TURNING INTA ALLIGATORS-
-AND SEEIN' INTA PEOPLE'S SOULS BY LOOKIN' THROUGH THE HOLE OF A DOUGHNUT.
I LISTEN CUZ HE GIVES ME FREE COOKIES SOMETIMES.
I USED TO THINK HE WAS CRAZY-

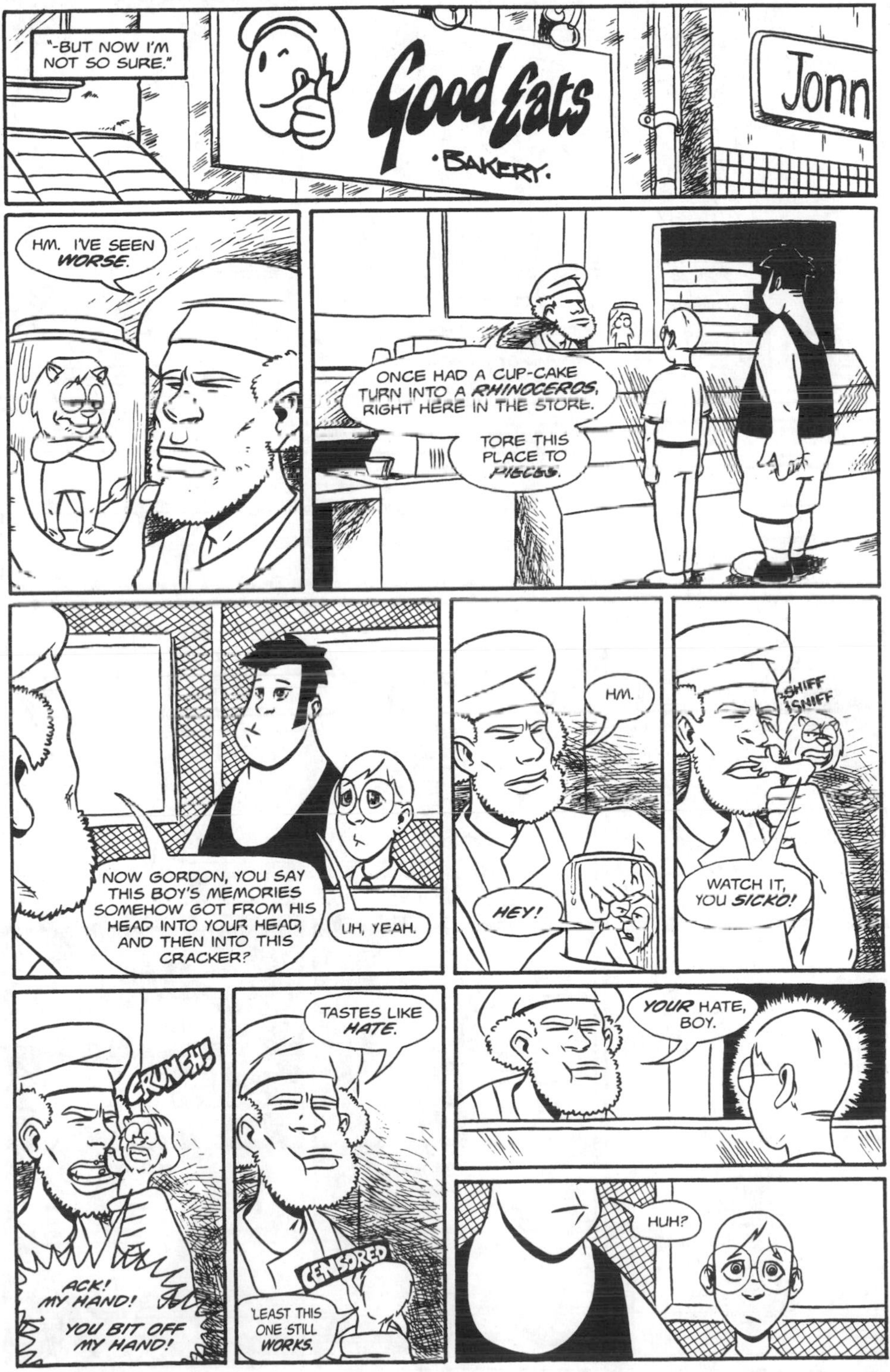
"-BUT NOW I'M NOT SO SURE."
Good Eats
·BAKERY·
Jonn
HM. I'VE SEEN WORSE.
ONCE HAD A CUP-CAKE TURN INTO A RHINOCEROS, RIGHT HERE IN THE STORE.
TORE THIS PLACE TO PIECES.
NOW GORDON, YOU SAY THIS BOY'S MEMORIES SOMEHOW GOT FROM HIS HEAD INTO YOUR HEAD, AND THEN INTO THIS CRACKER?
UH, YEAH.
HM.
HEY!
SNIFF SNIFF
WATCH IT, YOU SICKO!
CRUNCH!
ACK! MY HAND! YOU BIT OFF MY HAND!
TASTES LIKE HATE.
CENSORED
'LEAST THIS ONE STILL WORKS.
YOUR HATE, BOY.
HUH?

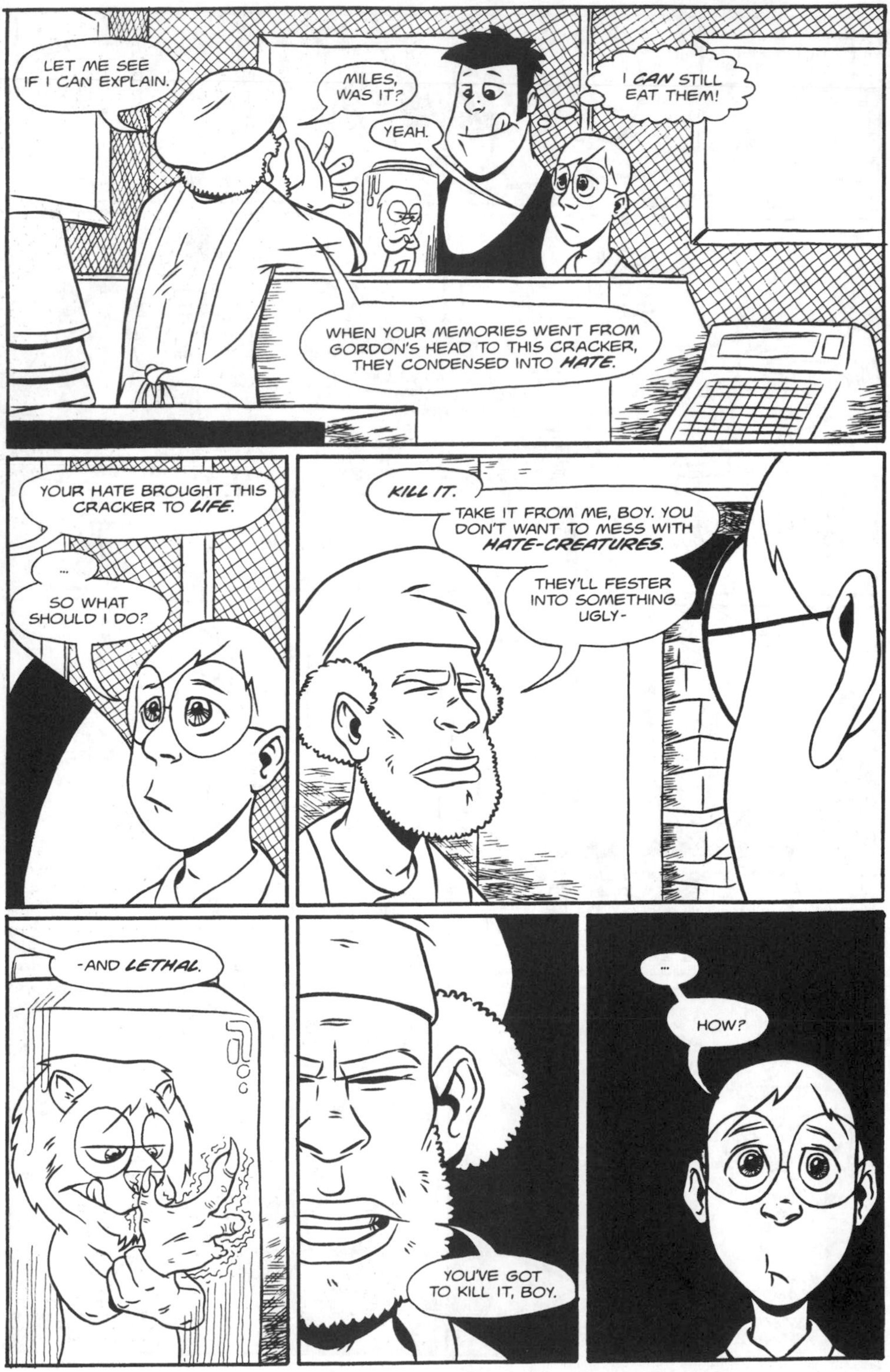
LET ME SEE IF I CAN EXPLAIN.
MILES, WAS IT?
YEAH.
I CAN STILL EAT THEM!
WHEN YOUR MEMORIES WENT FROM GORDON'S HEAD TO THIS CRACKER, THEY CONDENSED INTO HATE.
YOUR HATE BROUGHT THIS CRACKER TO LIFE.
...
SO WHAT SHOULD I DO?
KILL IT.
TAKE IT FROM ME, BOY. YOU DON'T WANT TO MESS WITH HATE-CREATURES.
THEY'LL FESTER INTO SOMETHING UGLY-
-AND LETHAL.
YOU'VE GOT TO KILL IT, BOY.
...
HOW?

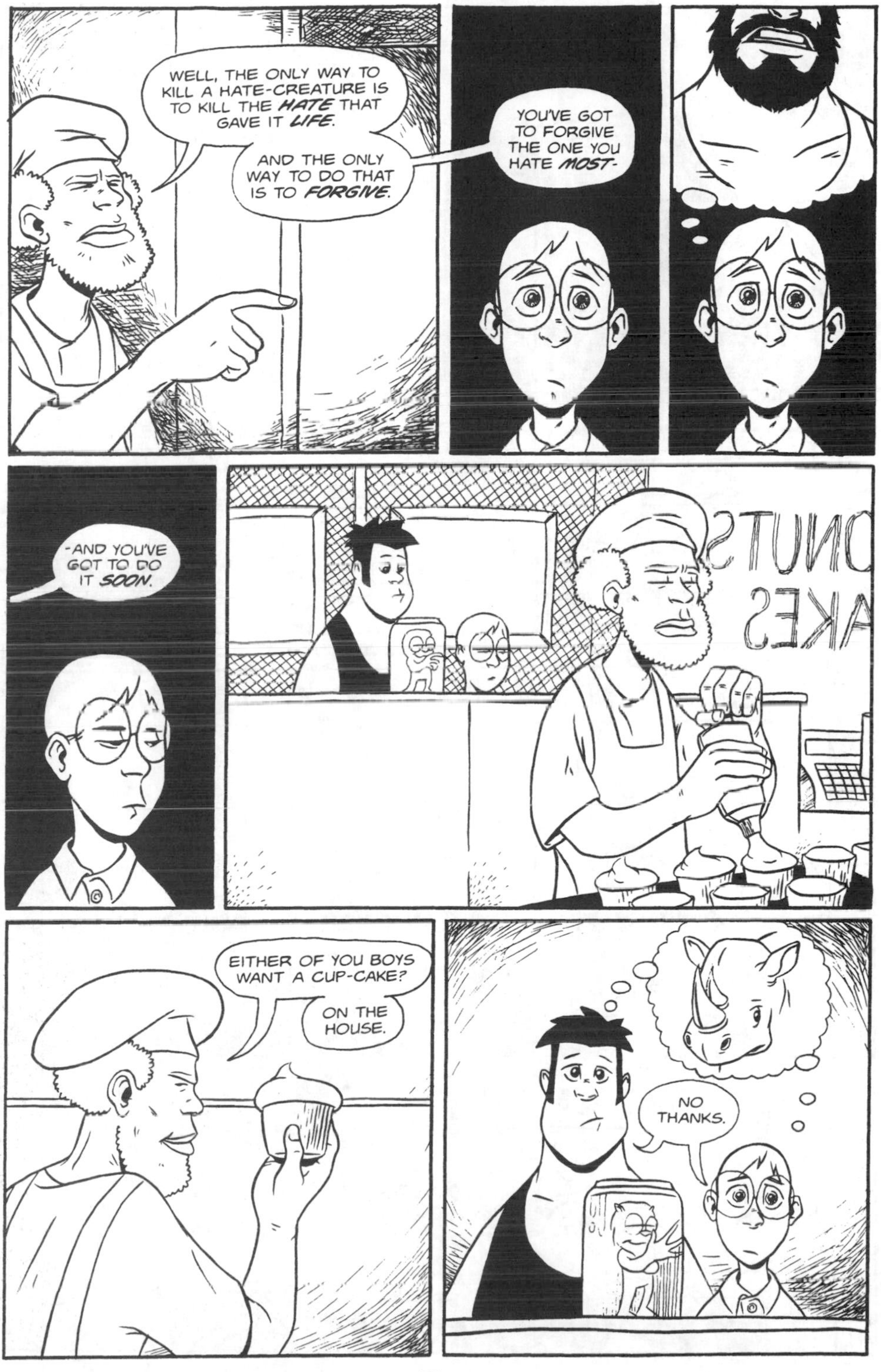
WELL, THE ONLY WAY TO KILL A HATE-CREATURE IS TO KILL THE HATE THAT GAVE IT LIFE.
AND THE ONLY WAY TO DO THAT IS TO FORGIVE.
YOU'VE GOT TO FORGIVE THE ONE YOU HATE MOST-
-AND YOU'VE GOT TO DO IT SOON.
ONUTS
AKES
EITHER OF YOU BOYS WANT A CUP-CAKE?
ON THE HOUSE.
NO THANKS.

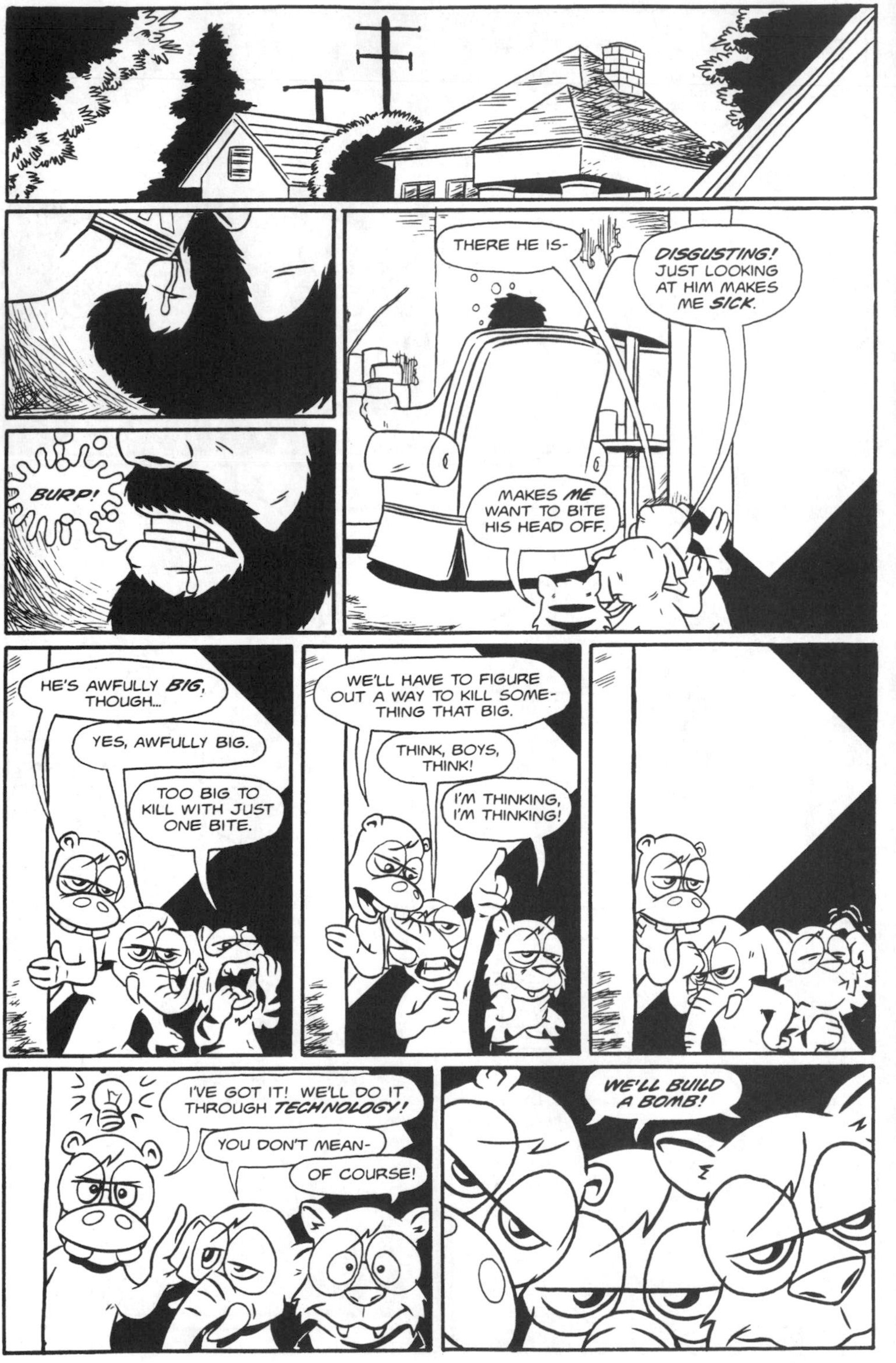
THERE HE IS-
DISGUSTING! JUST LOOKING AT HIM MAKES ME SICK.
BURP!
MAKES ME WANT TO BITE HIS HEAD OFF.
HE'S AWFULLY BIG, THOUGH...
YES, AWFULLY BIG.
TOO BIG TO KILL WITH JUST ONE BITE.
WE'LL HAVE TO FIGURE OUT A WAY TO KILL SOMETHING THAT BIG.
THINK, BOYS, THINK!
I'M THINKING, I'M THINKING!
I'VE GOT IT! WE'LL DO IT THROUGH TECHNOLOGY!
YOU DON'T MEAN-
OF COURSE!
WE'LL BUILD A BOMB!

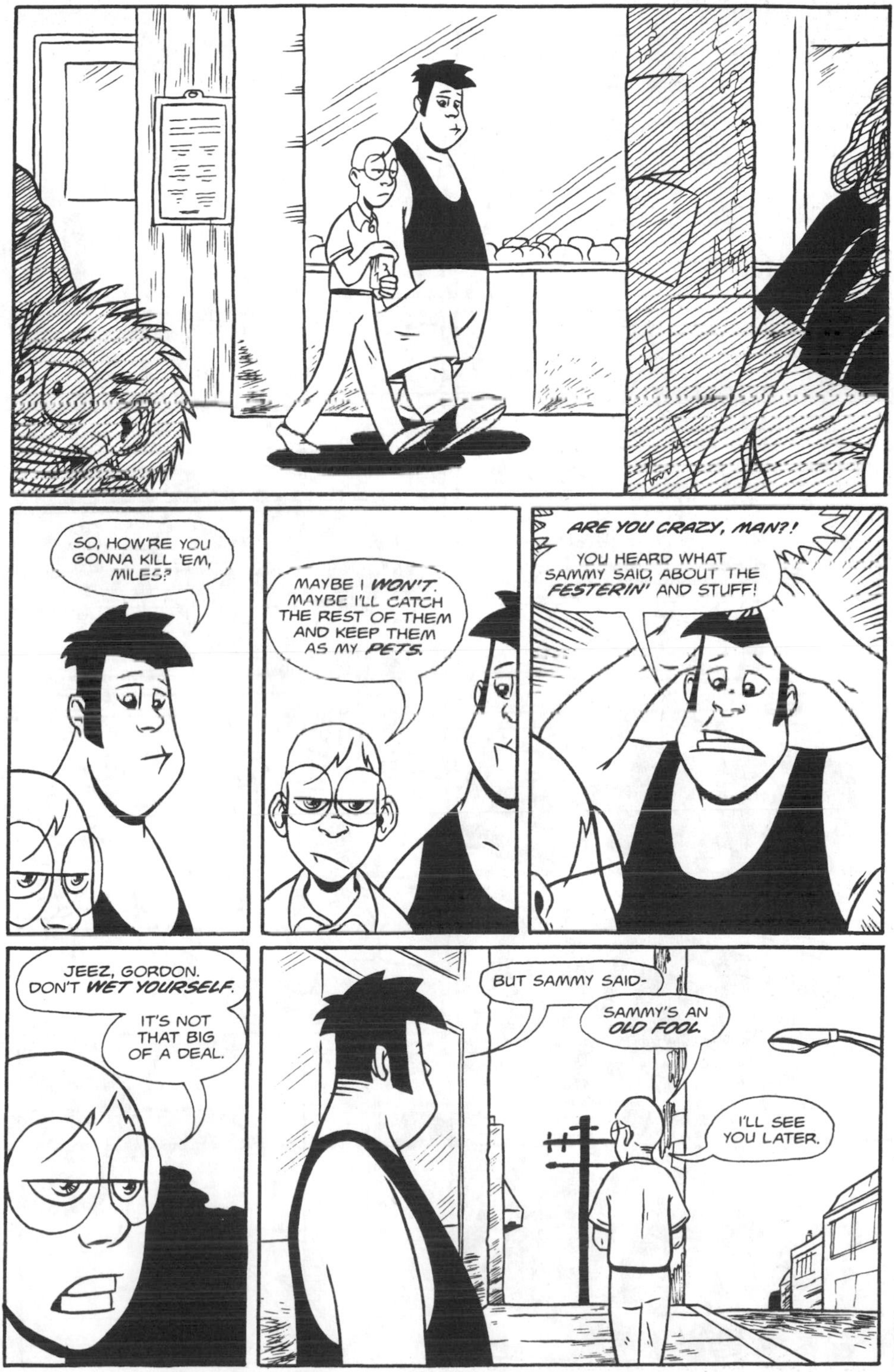
SO, HOW'RE YOU GONNA KILL 'EM, MILES?
MAYBE I WON'T. MAYBE I'LL CATCH THE REST OF THEM AND KEEP THEM AS MY PETS.
ARE YOU CRAZY, MAN?!
YOU HEARD WHAT SAMMY SAID, ABOUT THE FESTERIN' AND STUFF!
JEEZ, GORDON. DON'T WET YOURSELF.
IT'S NOT THAT BIG OF A DEAL.
BUT SAMMY SAID-
SAMMY'S AN OLD FOOL.
I'LL SEE YOU LATER.

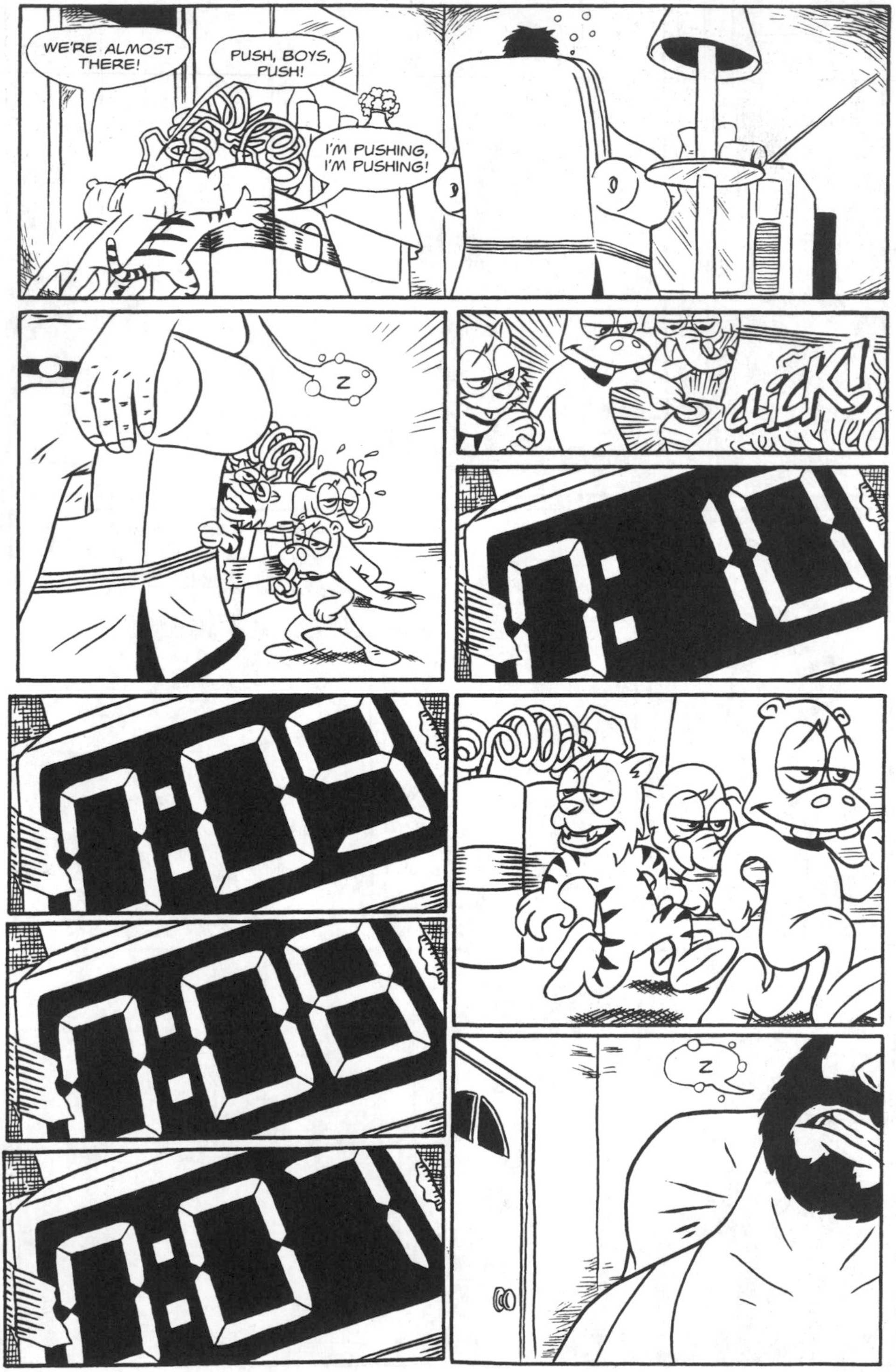
WE'RE ALMOST THERE!
PUSH, BOYS, PUSH!
I'M PUSHING, I'M PUSHING!
Z
CLICK!
Z

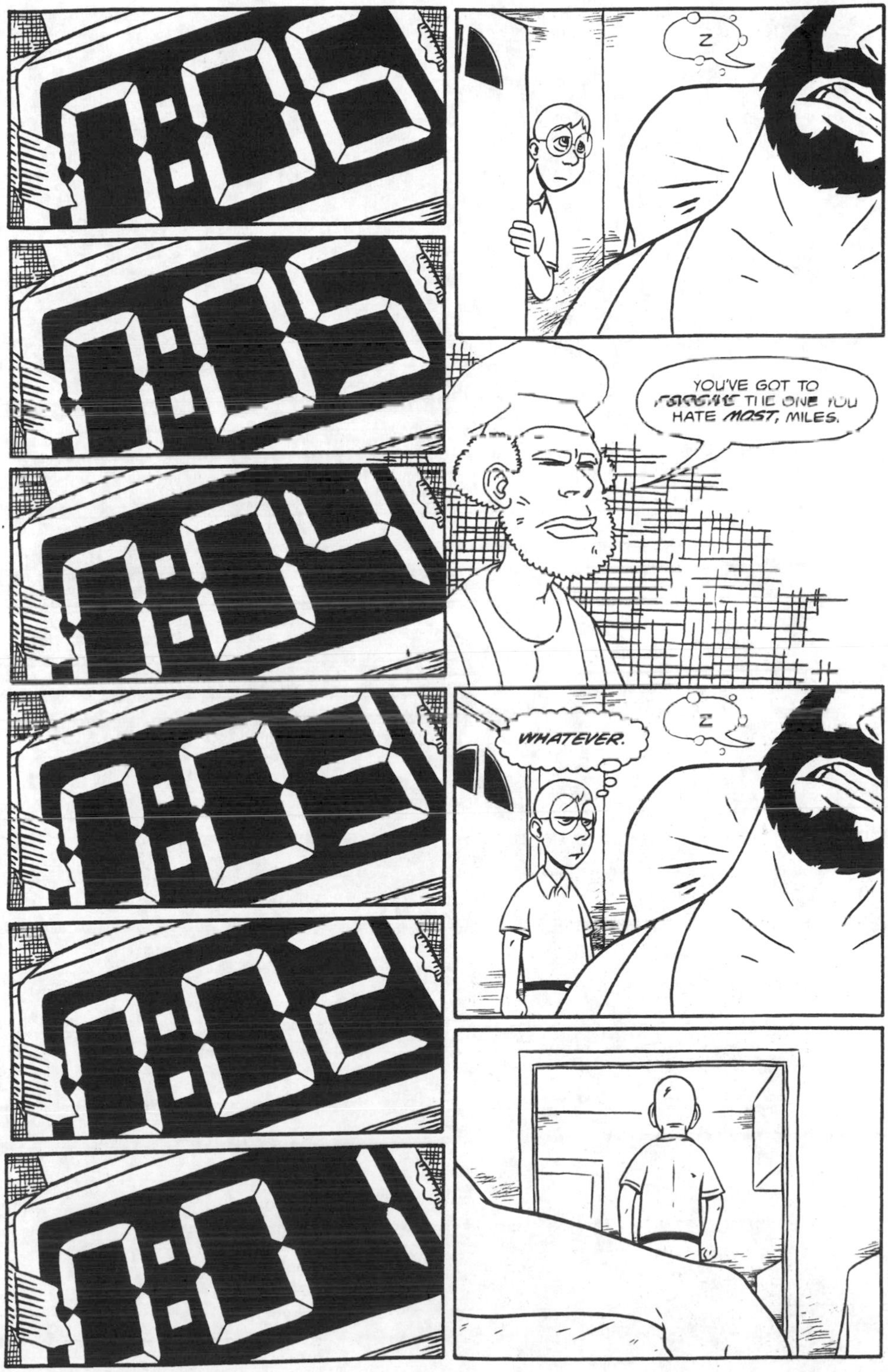
7:06
Z
7:05
YOU'VE GOT TO THE ONE YOU HATE *MOST*, MILES.
7:04
7:03
WHATEVER.
Z
7:02
7:01

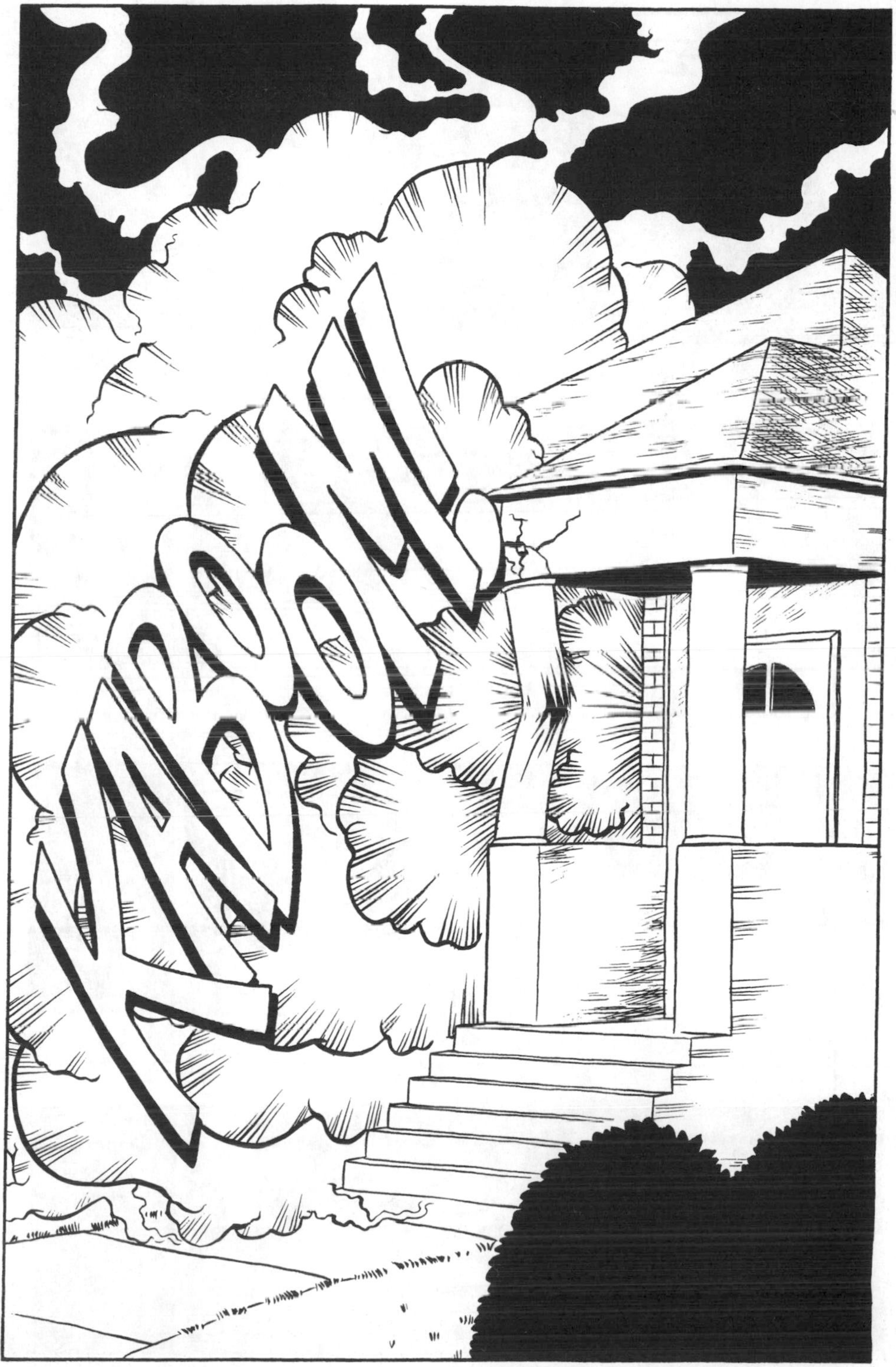
KABOOM!

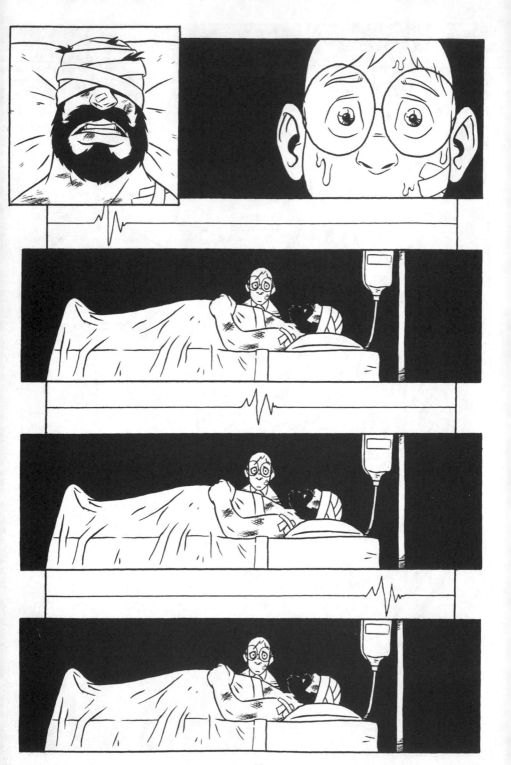

CHAPTER THREE

3

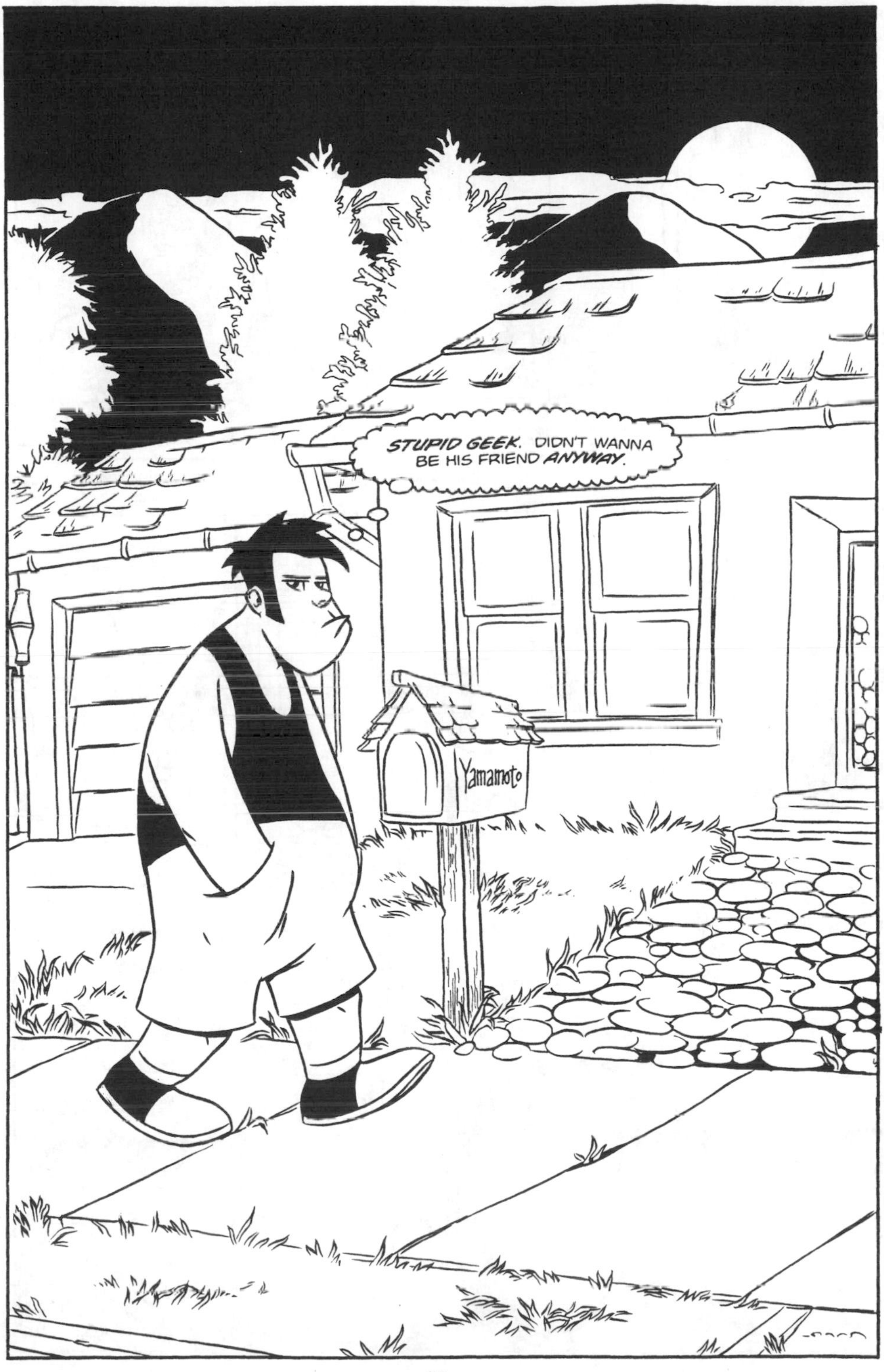
STUPID GEEK. DIDN'T WANNA BE HIS FRIEND ANYWAY.
Yamamoto

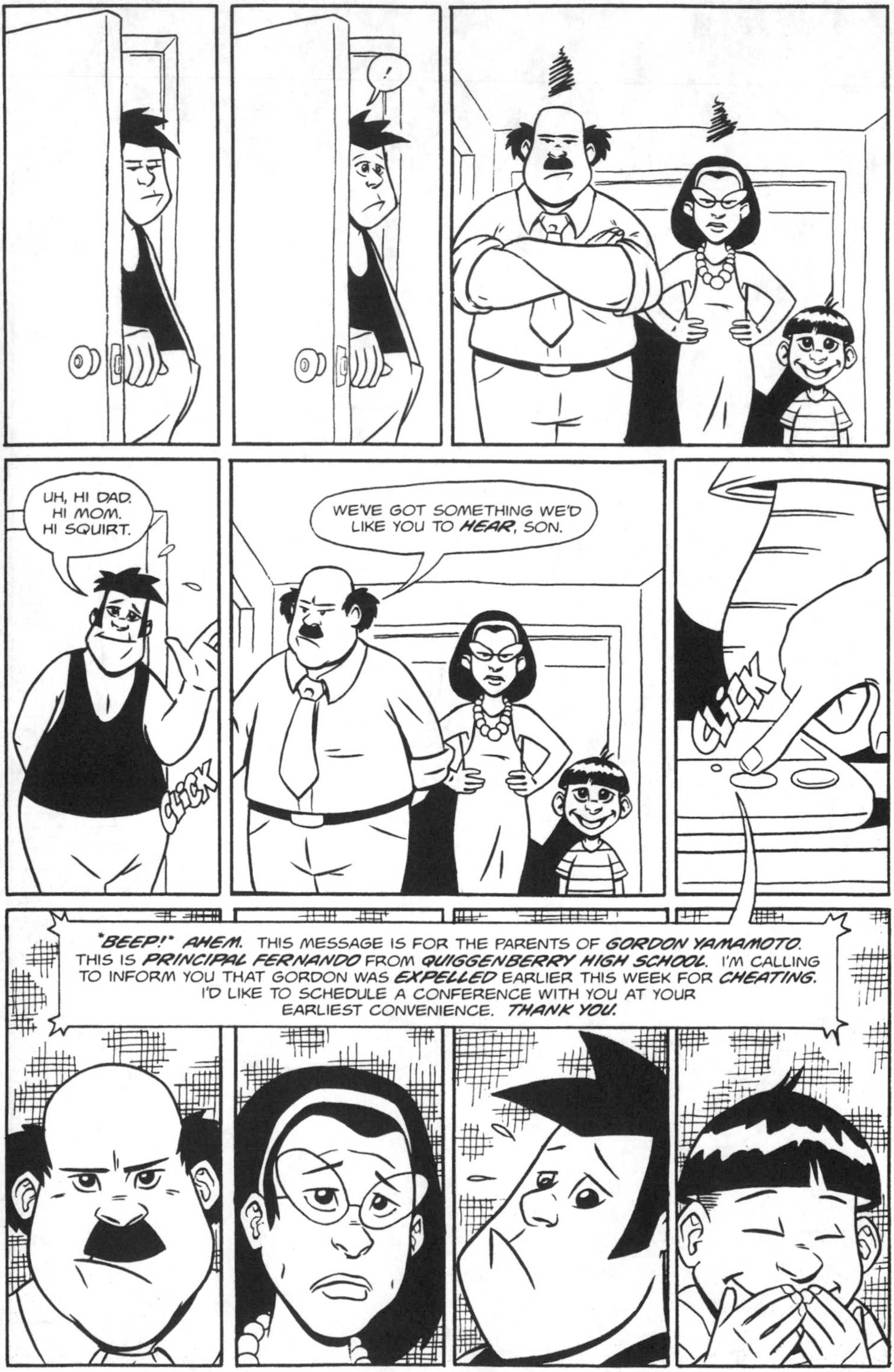
!
UH, HI DAD. HI MOM. HI SQUIRT.
CLICK
WE'VE GOT SOMETHING WE'D LIKE YOU TO HEAR, SON.
CLICK
BEEP! AHEM. THIS MESSAGE IS FOR THE PARENTS OF GORDON YAMAMOTO. THIS IS PRINCIPAL FERNANDO FROM QUIGGENBERRY HIGH SCHOOL. I'M CALLING TO INFORM YOU THAT GORDON WAS EXPELLED EARLIER THIS WEEK FOR CHEATING. I'D LIKE TO SCHEDULE A CONFERENCE WITH YOU AT YOUR EARLIEST CONVENIENCE. THANK YOU.

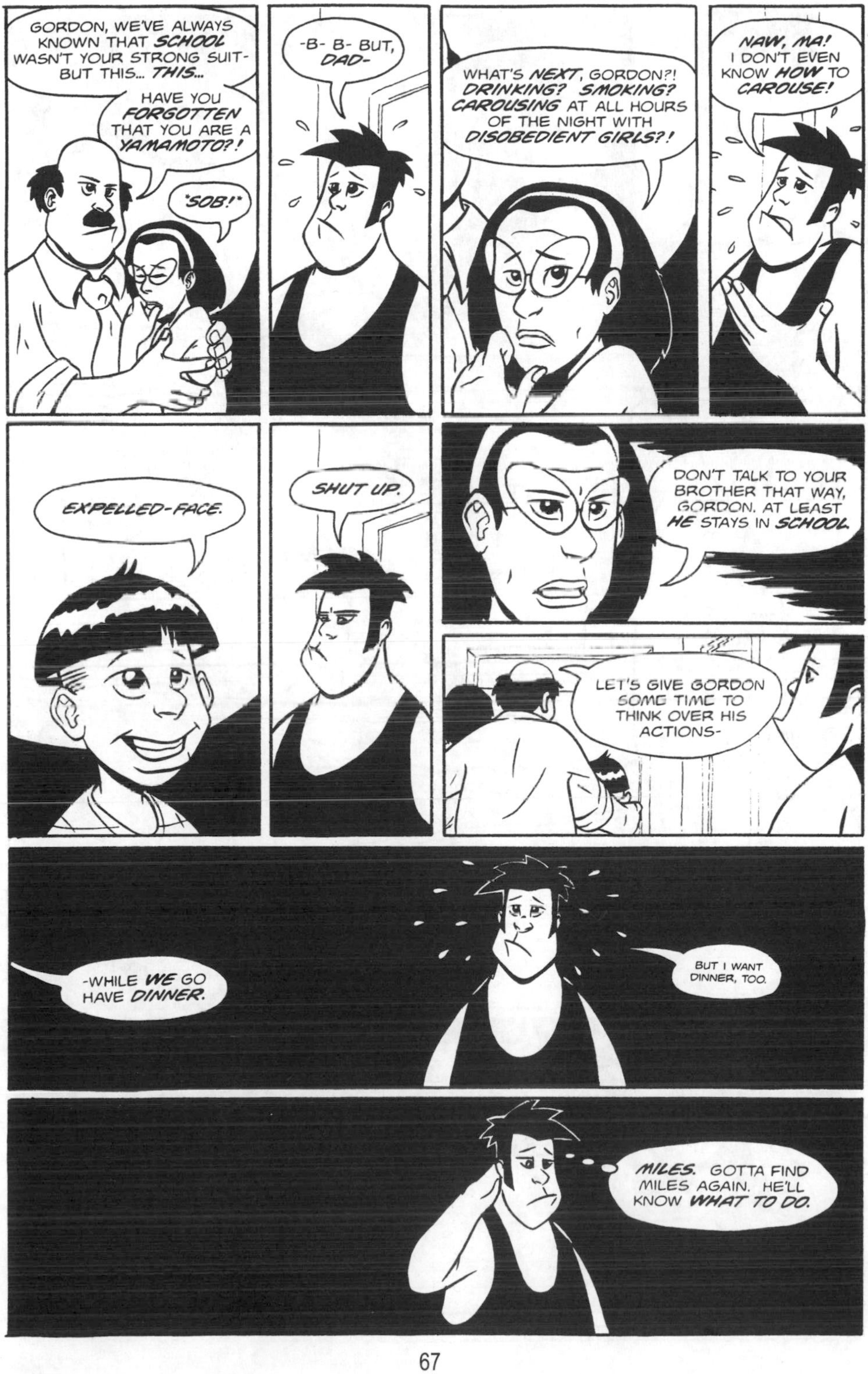
GORDON, WE'VE ALWAYS KNOWN THAT SCHOOL WASN'T YOUR STRONG SUIT- BUT THIS... THIS...
HAVE YOU FORGOTTEN THAT YOU ARE A YAMAMOTO?!
SOB!
-B- B- BUT, DAD-
WHAT'S NEXT, GORDON?! DRINKING? SMOKING? CAROUSING AT ALL HOURS OF THE NIGHT WITH DISOBEDIENT GIRLS?!
NAW, MA! I DON'T EVEN KNOW HOW TO CAROUSE!
EXPELLED-FACE.
SHUT UP.
DON'T TALK TO YOUR BROTHER THAT WAY, GORDON. AT LEAST HE STAYS IN SCHOOL.
LET'S GIVE GORDON SOME TIME TO THINK OVER HIS ACTIONS-
-WHILE WE GO HAVE DINNER.
BUT I WANT DINNER, TOO.
MILES. GOTTA FIND MILES AGAIN. HE'LL KNOW WHAT TO DO.

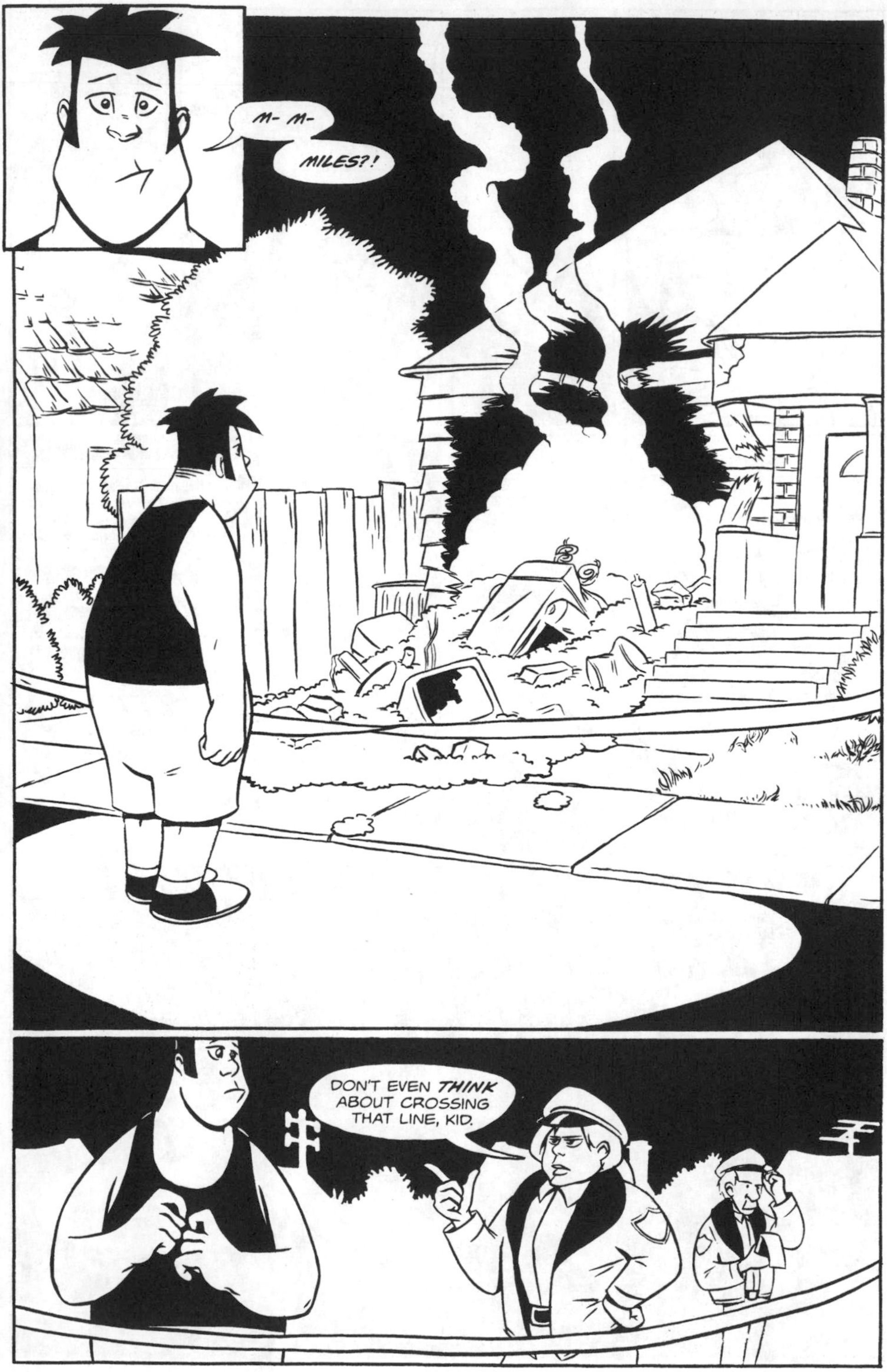
M- M-
MILES?!
DON'T EVEN *THINK* ABOUT CROSSING THAT LINE, KID.

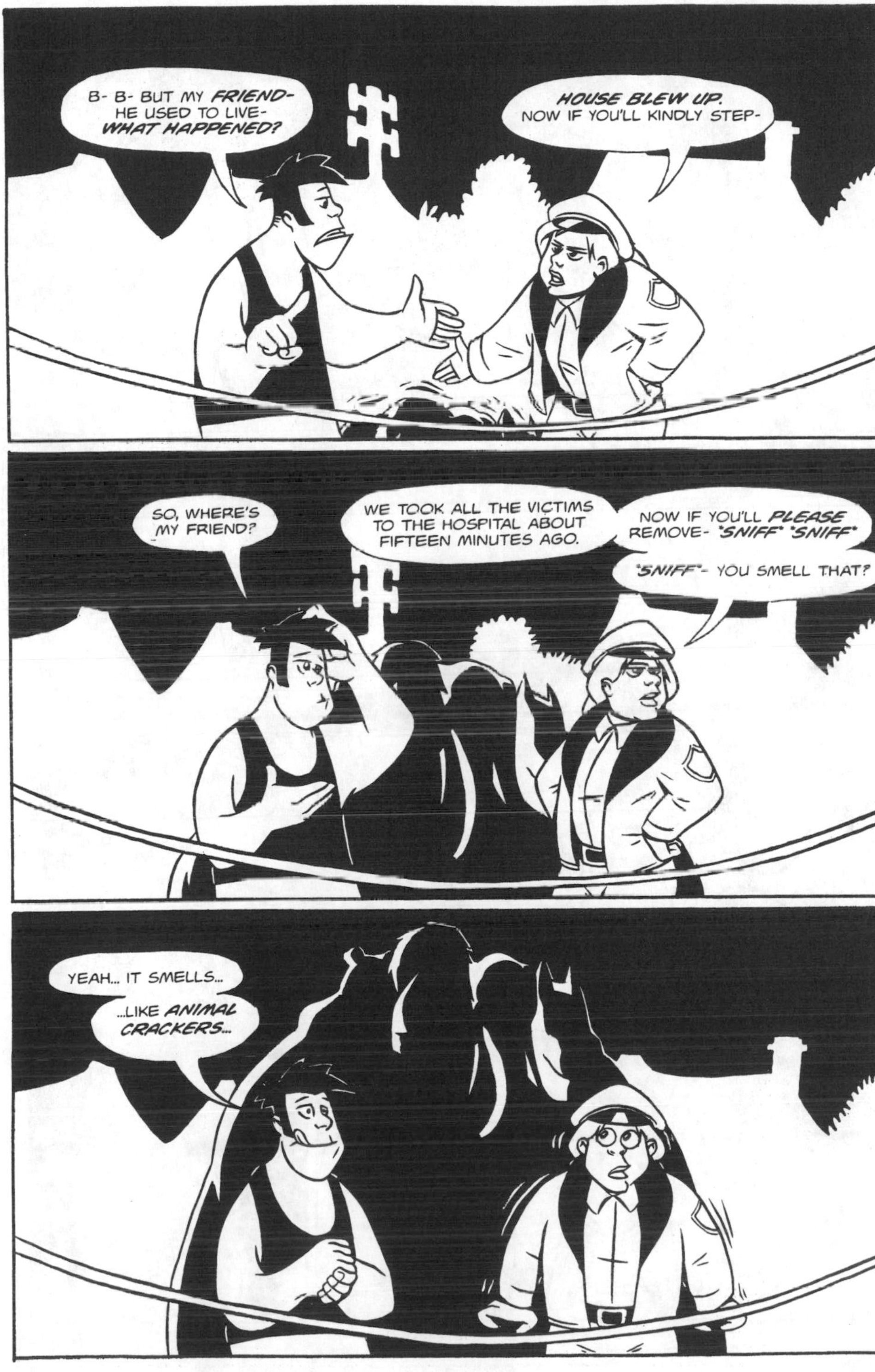
B- B- BUT MY FRIEND- HE USED TO LIVE- WHAT HAPPENED?
HOUSE BLEW UP. NOW IF YOU'LL KINDLY STEP-
SO, WHERE'S MY FRIEND?
WE TOOK ALL THE VICTIMS TO THE HOSPITAL ABOUT FIFTEEN MINUTES AGO.
NOW IF YOU'LL PLEASE REMOVE- *SNIFF* *SNIFF*
SNIFF- YOU SMELL THAT?
YEAH... IT SMELLS...
...LIKE ANIMAL CRACKERS...

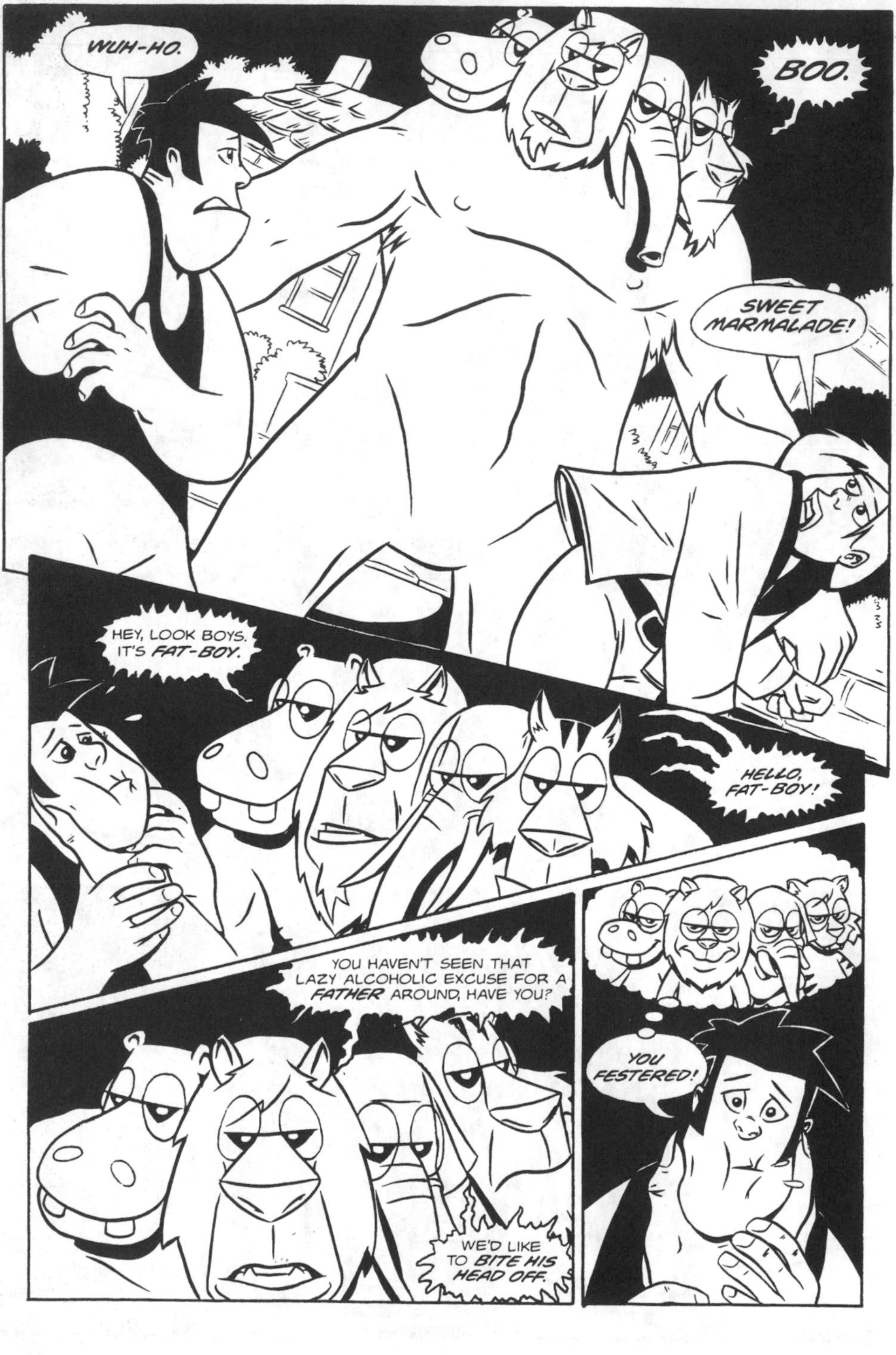
WUH-HO.
BOO.
SWEET MARMALADE!
HEY, LOOK BOYS. IT'S FAT-BOY.
HELLO, FAT-BOY!
YOU HAVEN'T SEEN THAT LAZY ALCOHOLIC EXCUSE FOR A FATHER AROUND, HAVE YOU?
WE'D LIKE TO BITE HIS HEAD OFF.
YOU FESTERED!

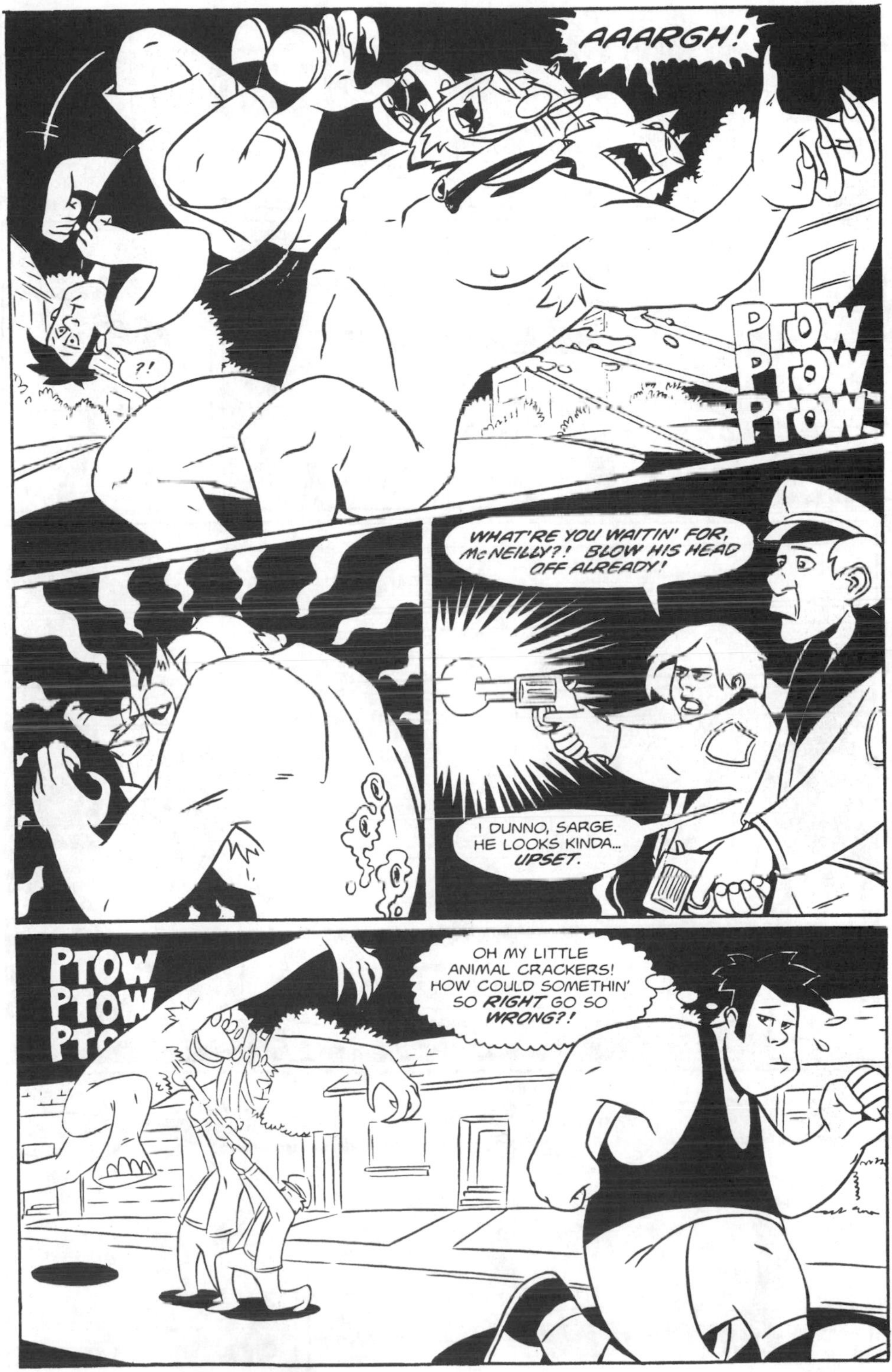
AAARGH!
?!
PTOW PTOW PTOW!
WHAT'RE YOU WAITIN' FOR, McNEILLY?! BLOW HIS HEAD OFF ALREADY!
I DUNNO, SARGE. HE LOOKS KINDA... UPSET.
PTOW PTOW PTO
OH MY LITTLE ANIMAL CRACKERS! HOW COULD SOMETHIN' SO RIGHT GO SO WRONG?!

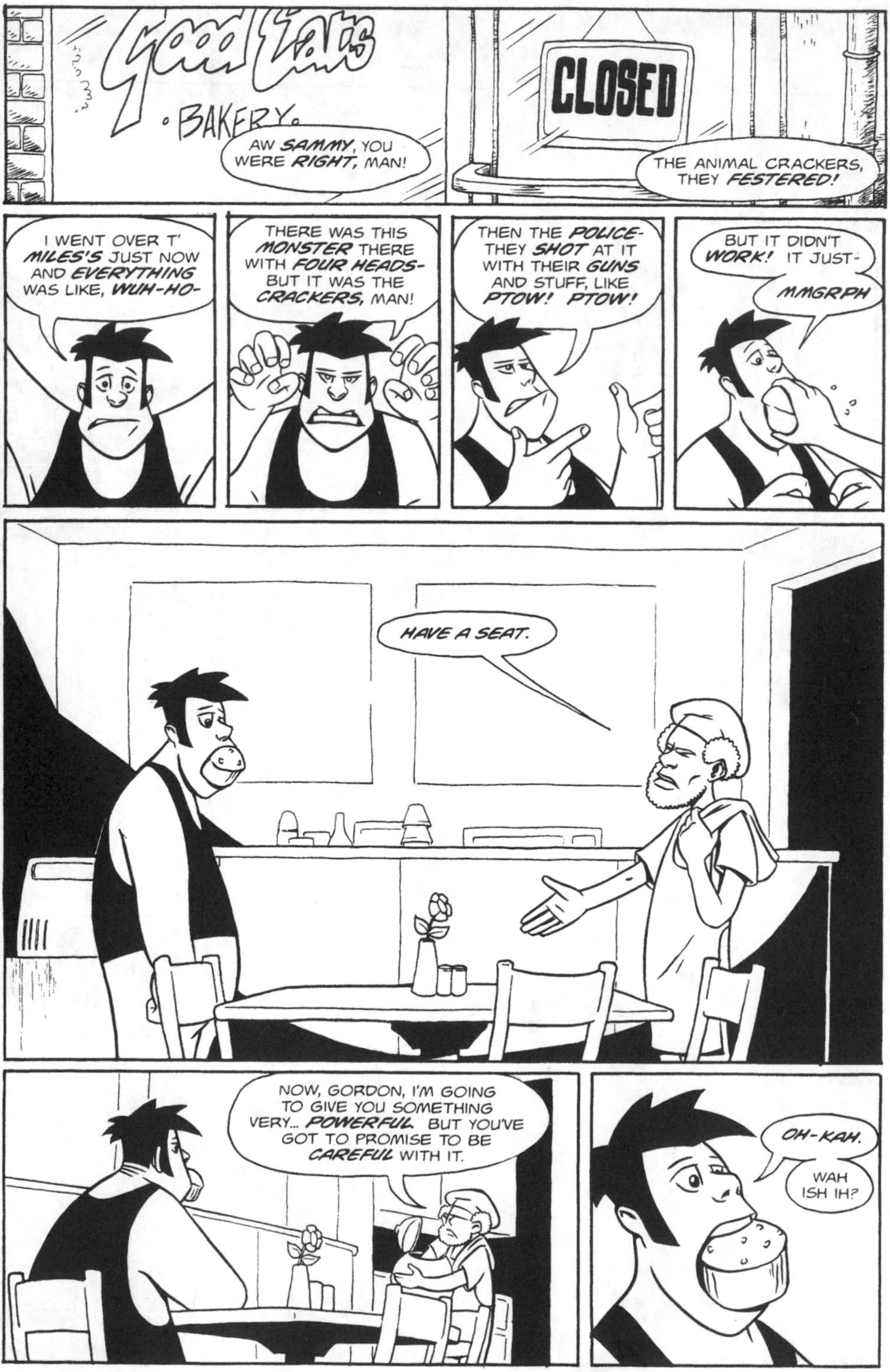
Good Eats
BAKERY
CLOSED
AW SAMMY, YOU WERE RIGHT, MAN!
THE ANIMAL CRACKERS, THEY FESTERED!
I WENT OVER T' MILES'S JUST NOW AND EVERYTHING WAS LIKE, WUH-HO-
THERE WAS THIS MONSTER THERE WITH FOUR HEADS- BUT IT WAS THE CRACKERS, MAN!
THEN THE POLICE- THEY SHOT AT IT WITH THEIR GUNS AND STUFF, LIKE PTOW! PTOW!
BUT IT DIDN'T WORK! IT JUST-
MMGRPH
HAVE A SEAT.
NOW, GORDON, I'M GOING TO GIVE YOU SOMETHING VERY... POWERFUL. BUT YOU'VE GOT TO PROMISE TO BE CAREFUL WITH IT.
OH-KAH.
WAH ISH IH?

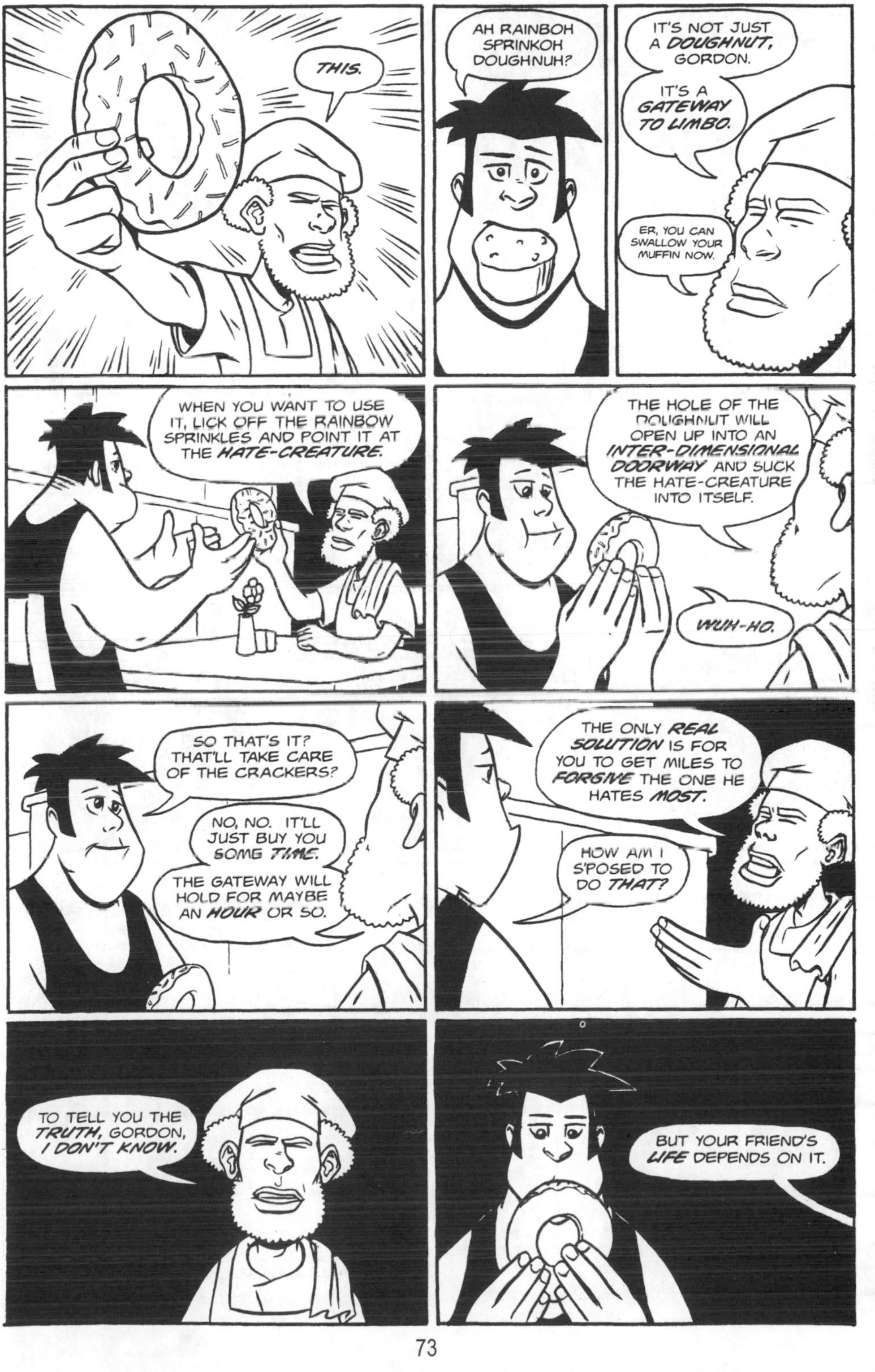
THIS.
AH RAINBOH SPRINKOH DOUGHNUH?
IT'S NOT JUST A DOUGHNUT, GORDON.
IT'S A GATEWAY TO LIMBO.
ER, YOU CAN SWALLOW YOUR MUFFIN NOW.
WHEN YOU WANT TO USE IT, LICK OFF THE RAINBOW SPRINKLES AND POINT IT AT THE HATE-CREATURE.
THE HOLE OF THE DOUGHNUT WILL OPEN UP INTO AN INTER-DIMENSIONAL DOORWAY AND SUCK THE HATE-CREATURE INTO ITSELF.
WUH-HO.
SO THAT'S IT? THAT'LL TAKE CARE OF THE CRACKERS?
NO, NO. IT'LL JUST BUY YOU SOME TIME.
THE GATEWAY WILL HOLD FOR MAYBE AN HOUR OR SO.
THE ONLY REAL SOLUTION IS FOR YOU TO GET MILES TO FORGIVE THE ONE HE HATES MOST.
HOW AM I S'POSED TO DO THAT?
TO TELL YOU THE TRUTH, GORDON, I DON'T KNOW.
BUT YOUR FRIEND'S LIFE DEPENDS ON IT.

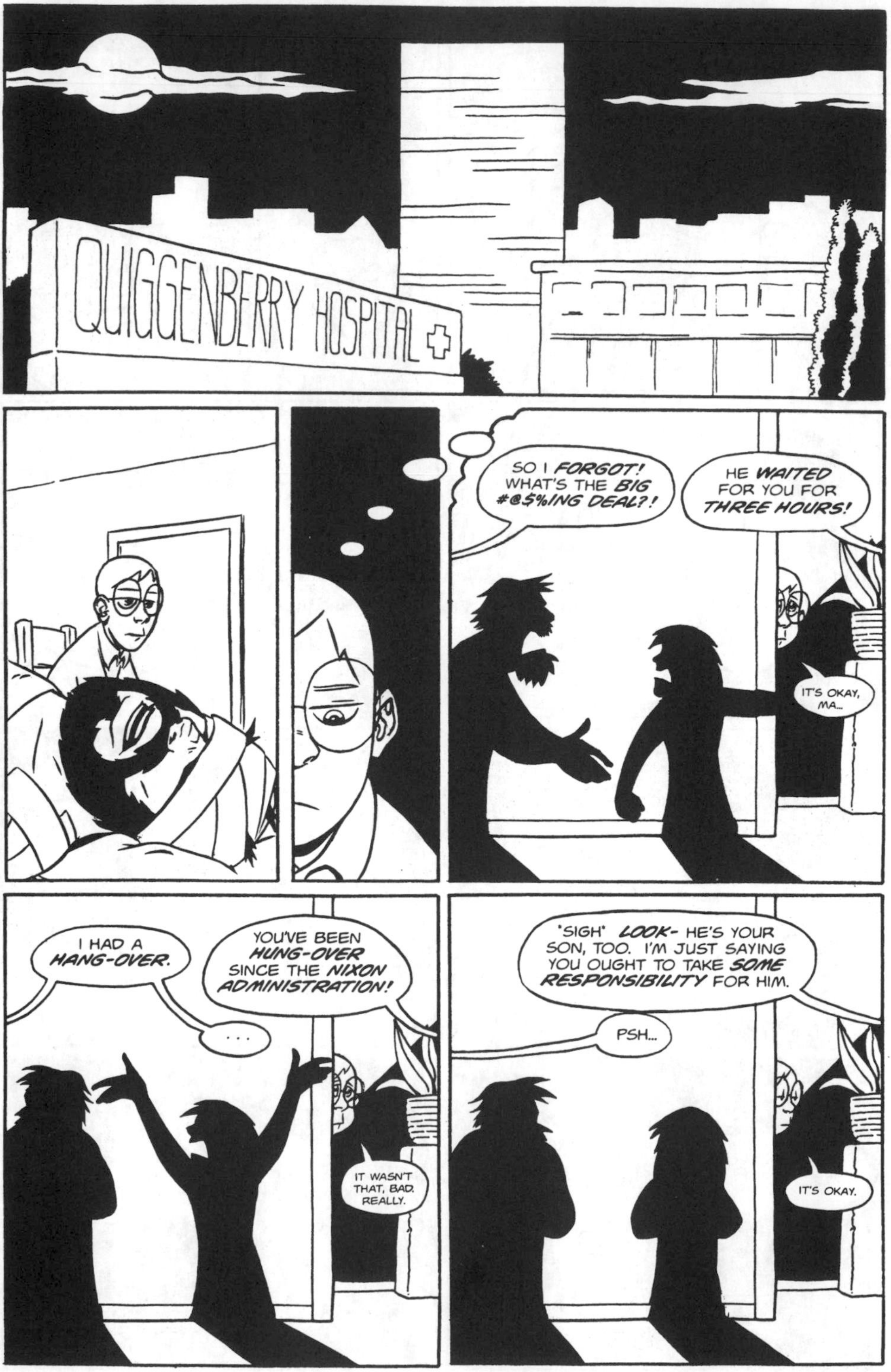
QUIGGENBERRY HOSPITAL
SO I FORGOT! WHAT'S THE BIG #@$%ING DEAL?!
HE WAITED FOR YOU FOR THREE HOURS!
IT'S OKAY, MA...
I HAD A HANG-OVER.
YOU'VE BEEN HUNG-OVER SINCE THE NIXON ADMINISTRATION!
. . .
IT WASN'T THAT, BAD. REALLY.
'SIGH' LOOK- HE'S YOUR SON, TOO. I'M JUST SAYING YOU OUGHT TO TAKE SOME RESPONSIBILITY FOR HIM.
PSH...
IT'S OKAY.

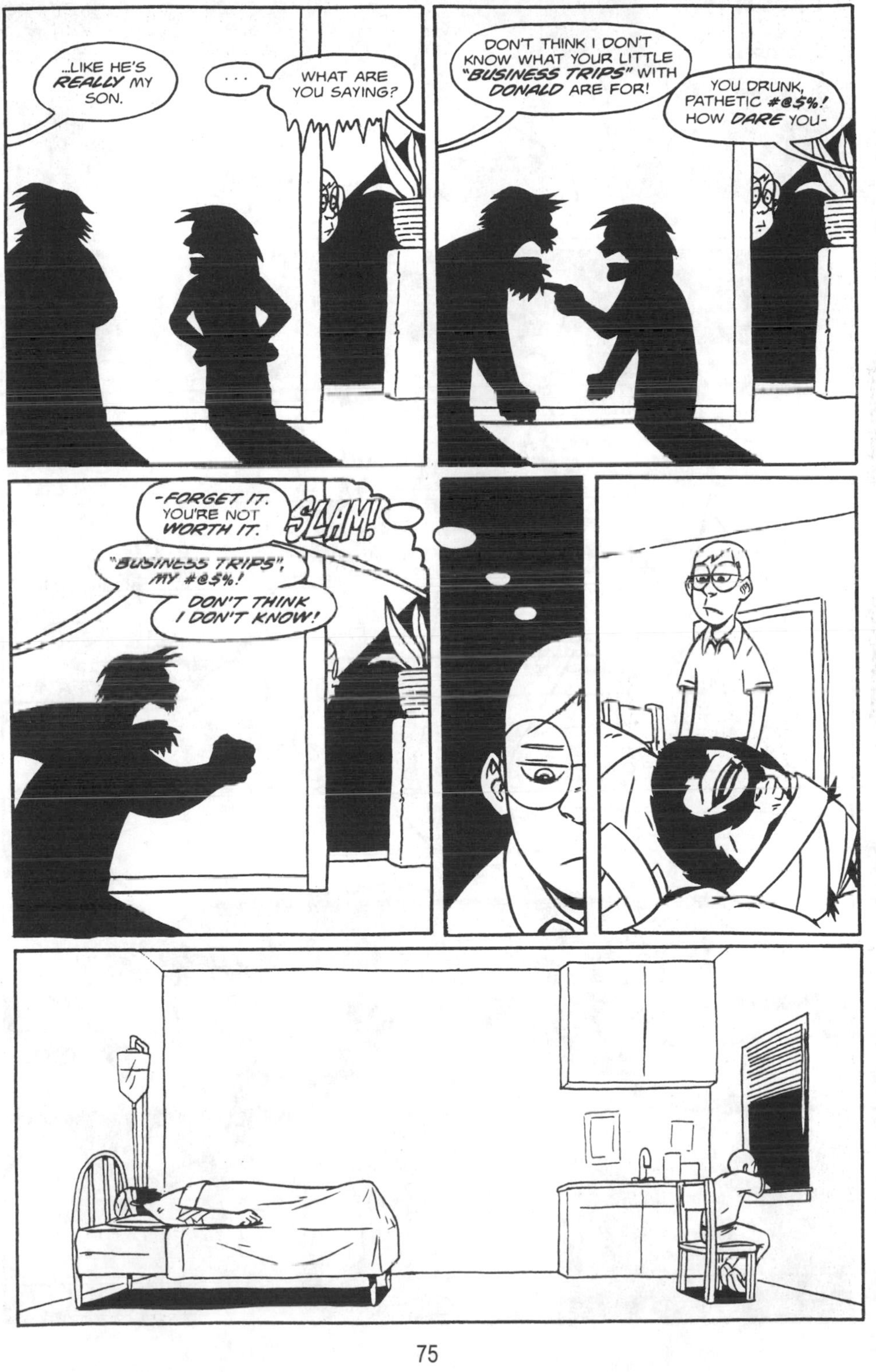
...LIKE HE'S REALLY MY SON.
...
WHAT ARE YOU SAYING?
DON'T THINK I DON'T KNOW WHAT YOUR LITTLE "BUSINESS TRIPS" WITH DONALD ARE FOR!
YOU DRUNK, PATHETIC #@$%! HOW DARE YOU-
-FORGET IT. YOU'RE NOT WORTH IT.
SLAM!
"BUSINESS TRIPS", MY #@$%!
DON'T THINK I DON'T KNOW!

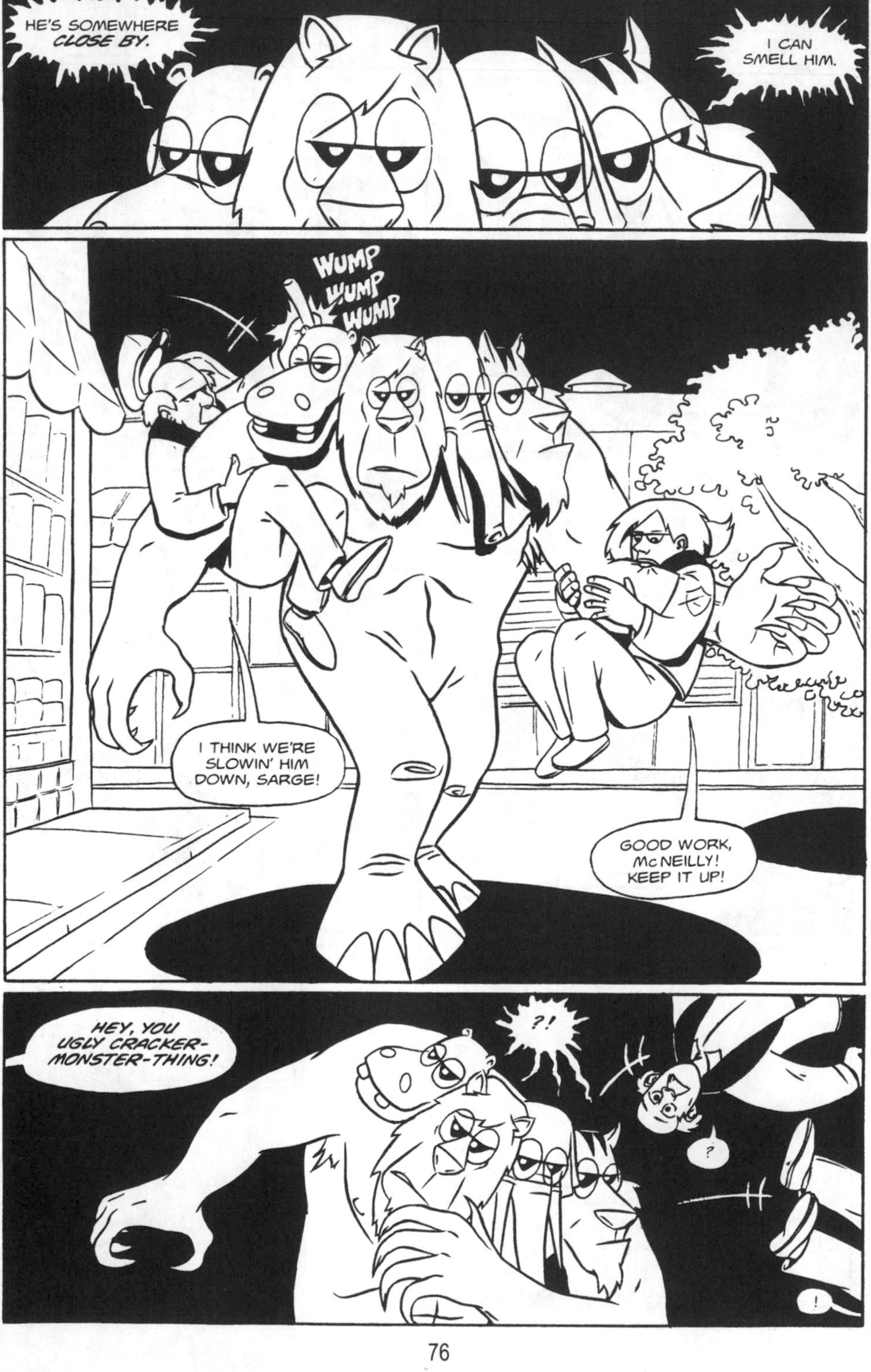
HE'S SOMEWHERE CLOSE BY.
I CAN SMELL HIM.
WUMP WUMP WUMP
I THINK WE'RE SLOWIN' HIM DOWN, SARGE!
GOOD WORK, McNEILLY! KEEP IT UP!
HEY, YOU UGLY CRACKER-MONSTER-THING!
?!
?
!

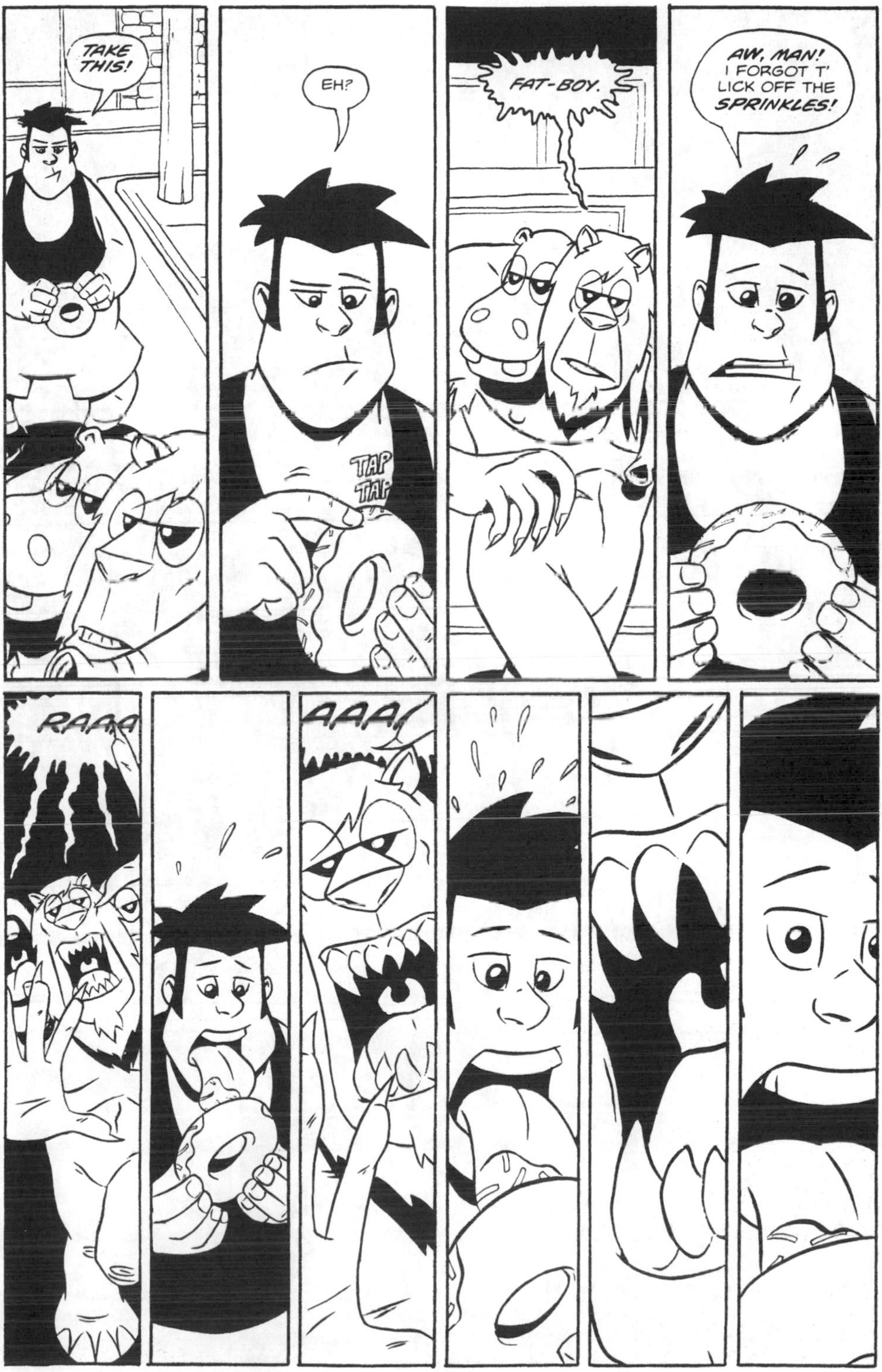
TAKE THIS!
EH?
TAP TAP
FAT-BOY.
AW, MAN! I FORGOT T' LICK OFF THE SPRINKLES!
RAAA
AAA!

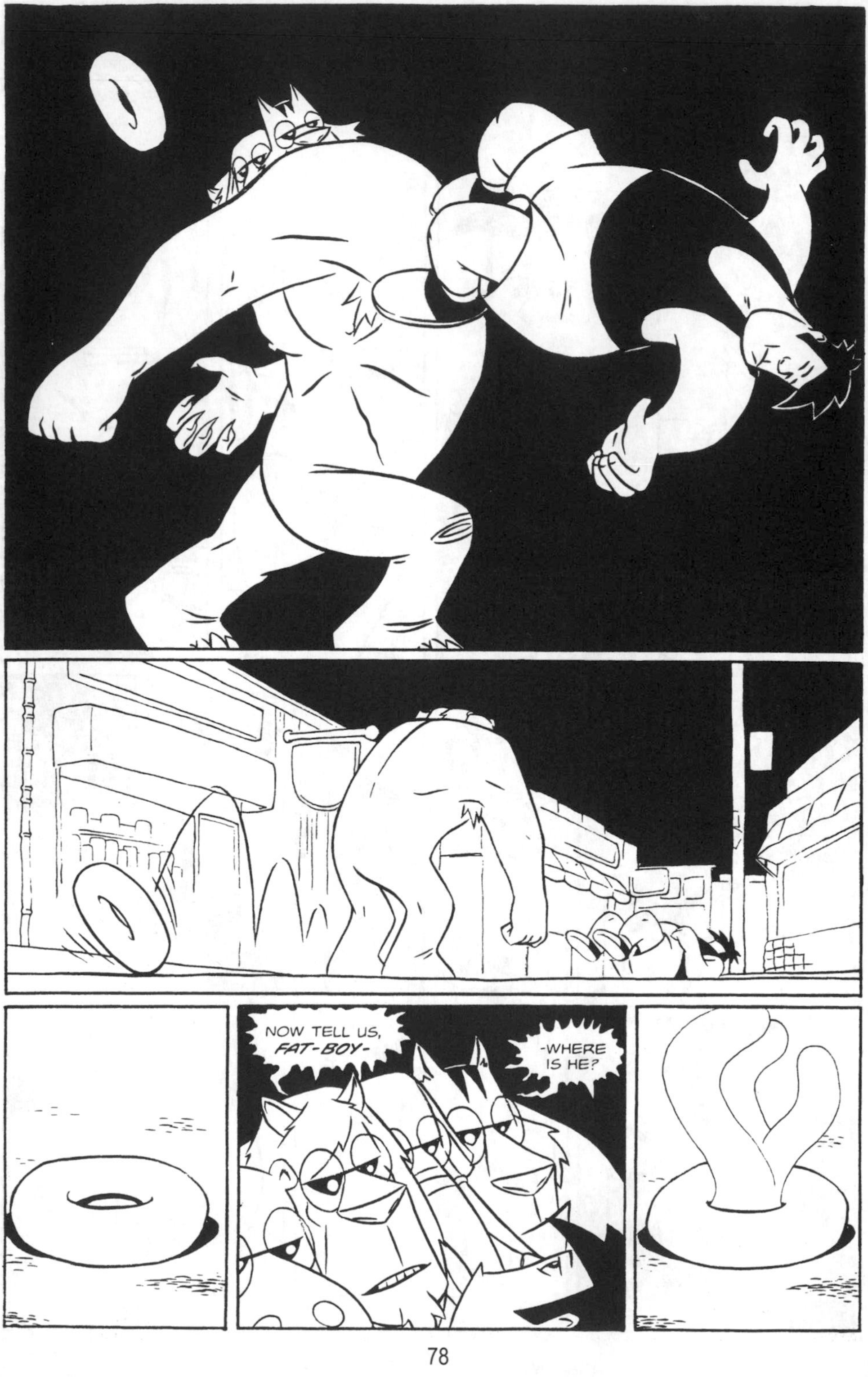
NOW TELL US, *FAT-BOY-*
-WHERE IS HE?

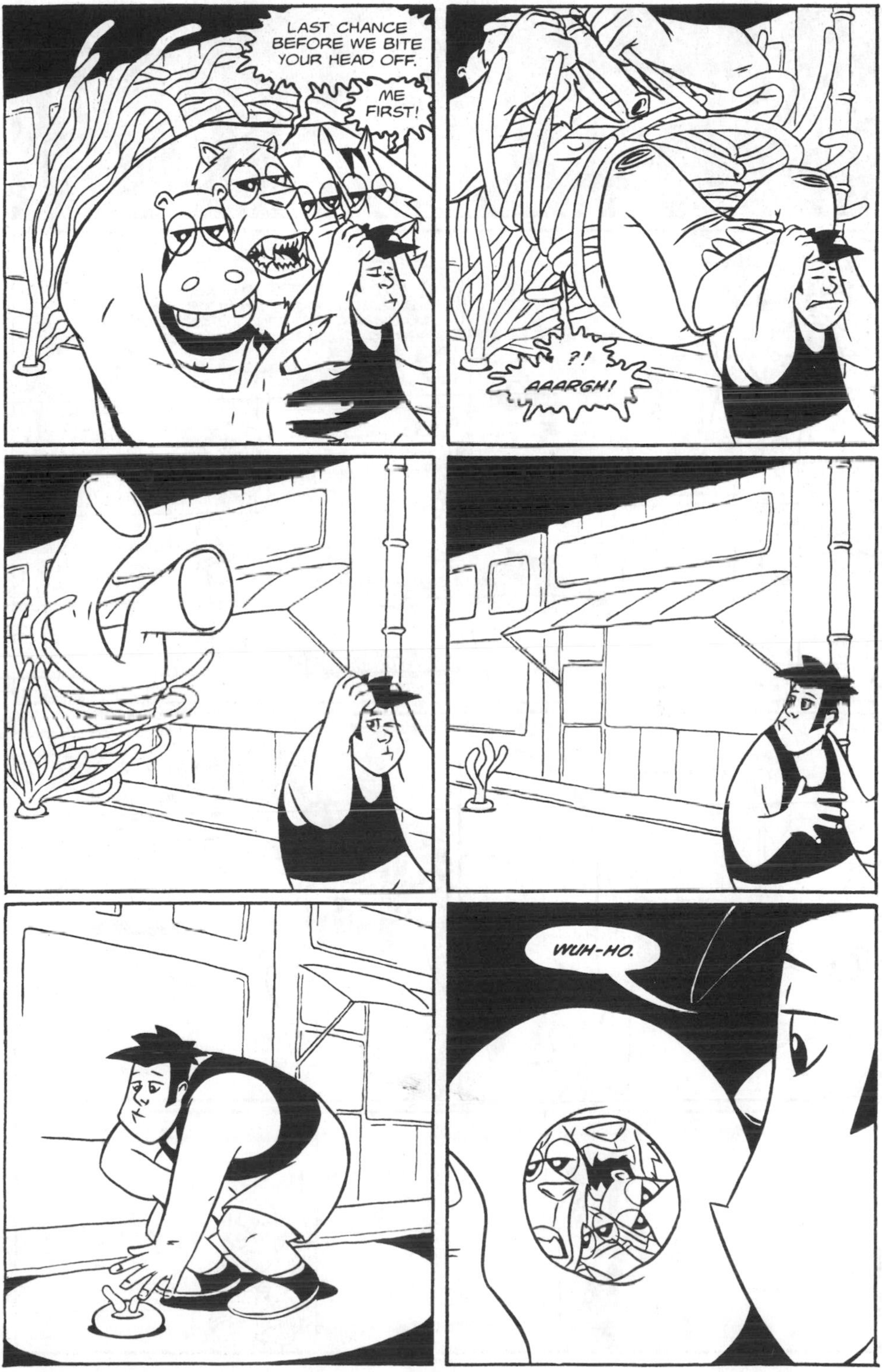
LAST CHANCE BEFORE WE BITE YOUR HEAD OFF.
ME FIRST!
?!
AAARGH!
WUH-HO.

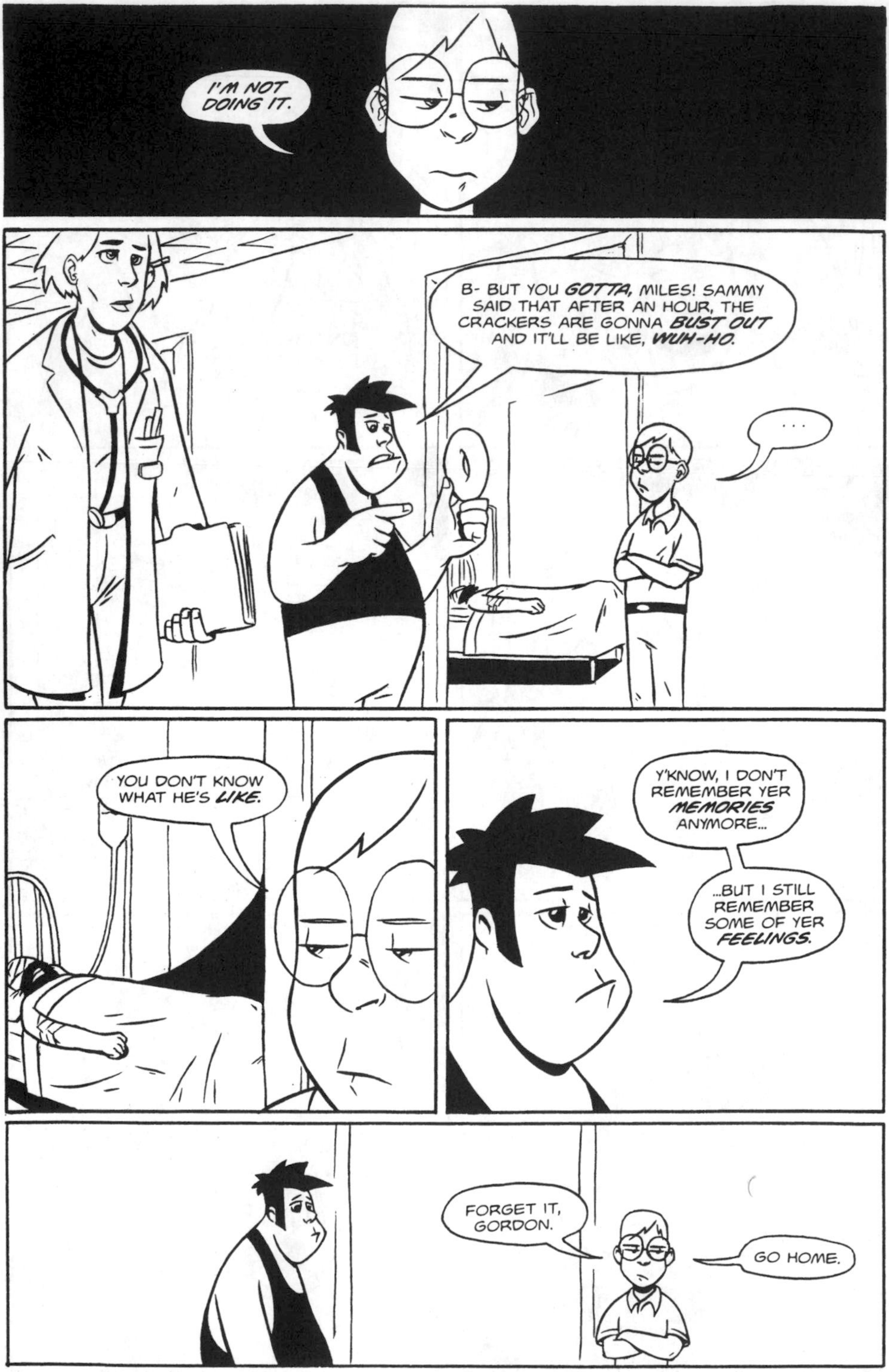
I'M NOT DOING IT.
B- BUT YOU GOTTA, MILES! SAMMY SAID THAT AFTER AN HOUR, THE CRACKERS ARE GONNA BUST OUT AND IT'LL BE LIKE, WUH-HO.
. . .
YOU DON'T KNOW WHAT HE'S LIKE.
Y'KNOW, I DON'T REMEMBER YER MEMORIES ANYMORE...
...BUT I STILL REMEMBER SOME OF YER FEELINGS.
FORGET IT, GORDON.
GO HOME.

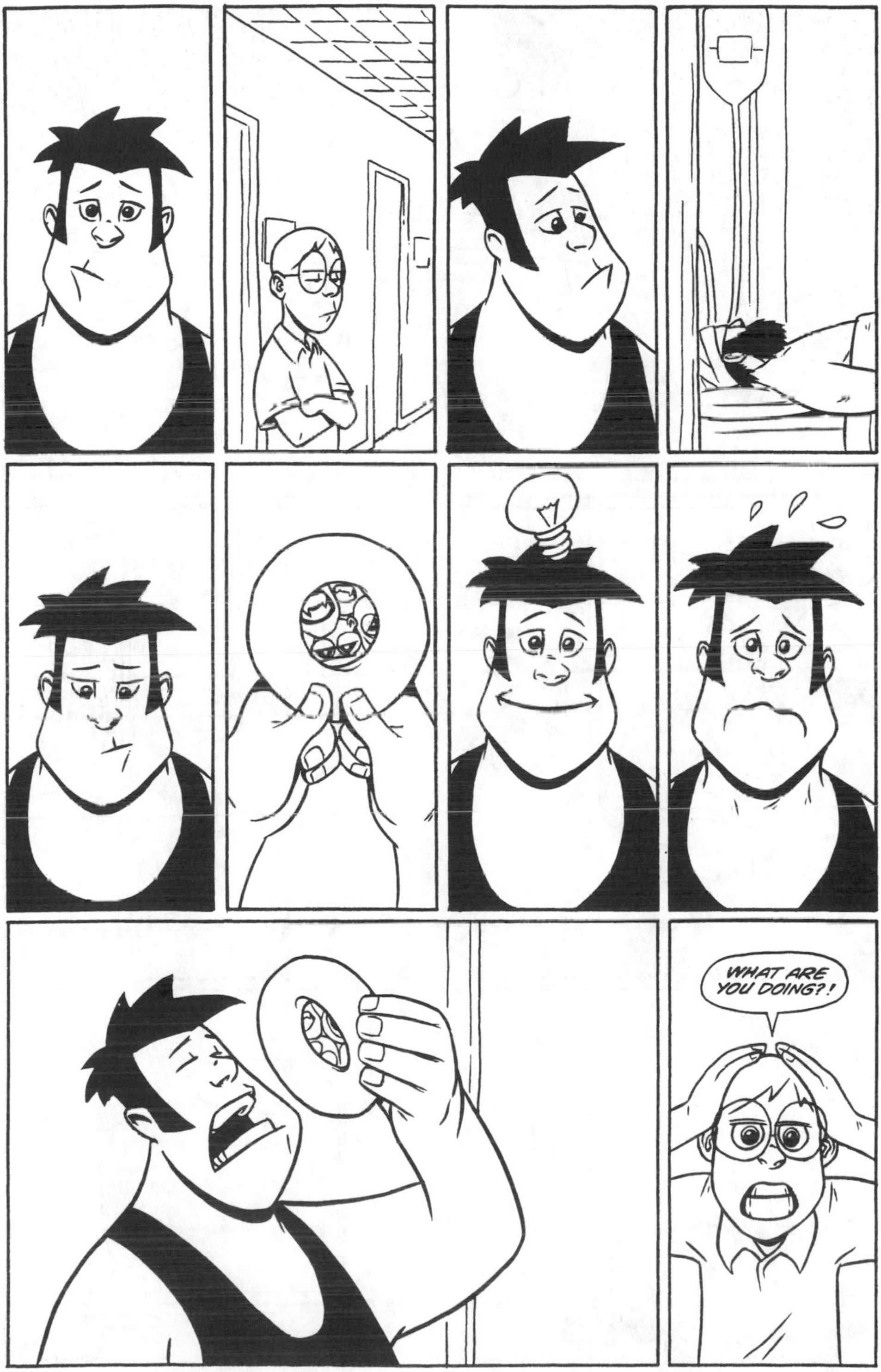
WHAT ARE YOU DOING?!

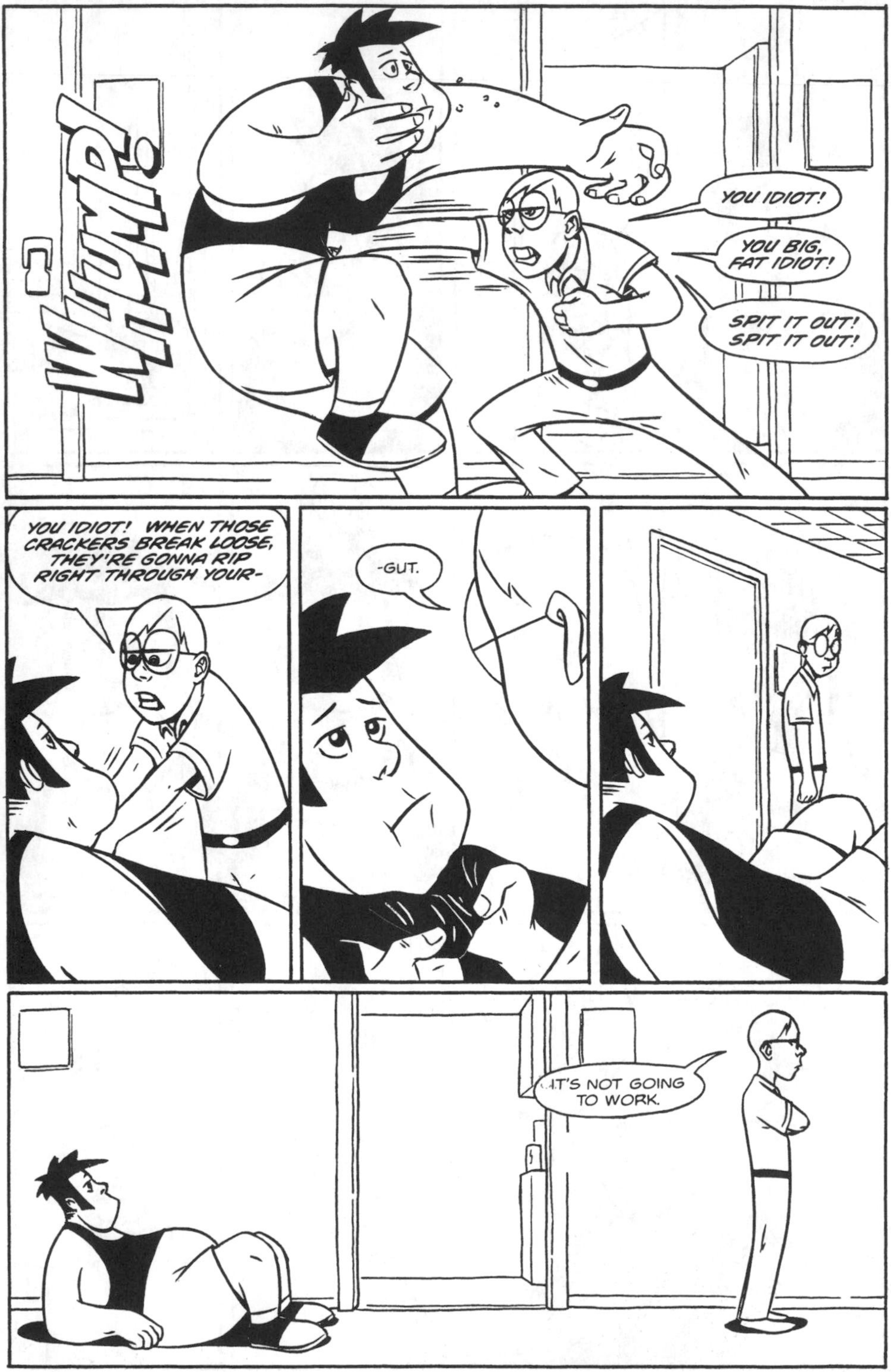
WHUMP!
YOU IDIOT!
YOU BIG, FAT IDIOT!
SPIT IT OUT! SPIT IT OUT!
YOU IDIOT! WHEN THOSE CRACKERS BREAK LOOSE, THEY'RE GONNA RIP RIGHT THROUGH YOUR-
-GUT.
IT'S NOT GOING TO WORK.

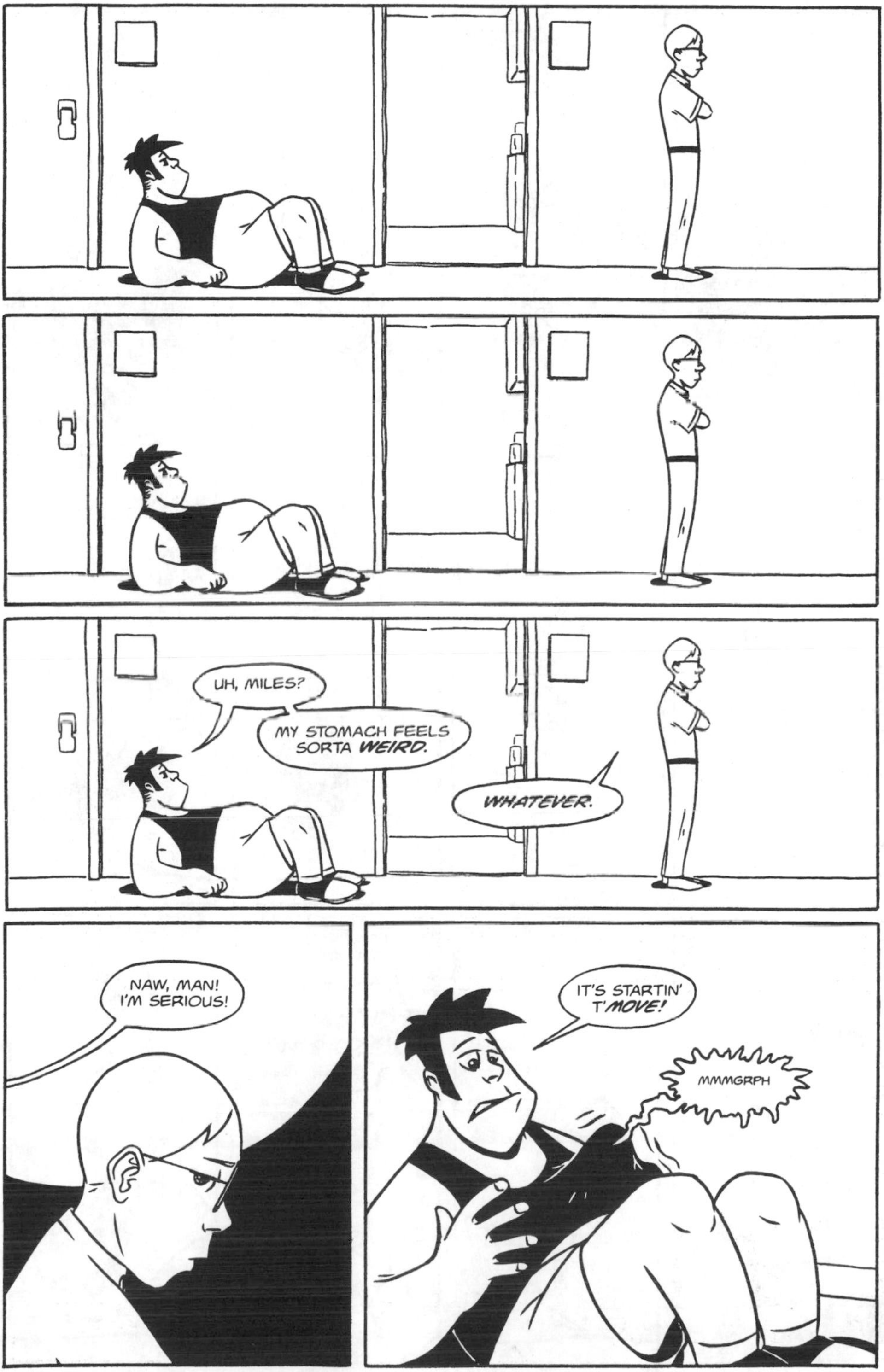
UH, MILES?
MY STOMACH FEELS SORTA WEIRD.
WHATEVER.
NAW, MAN! I'M SERIOUS!
IT'S STARTIN' T'MOVE!
MMMGRPH

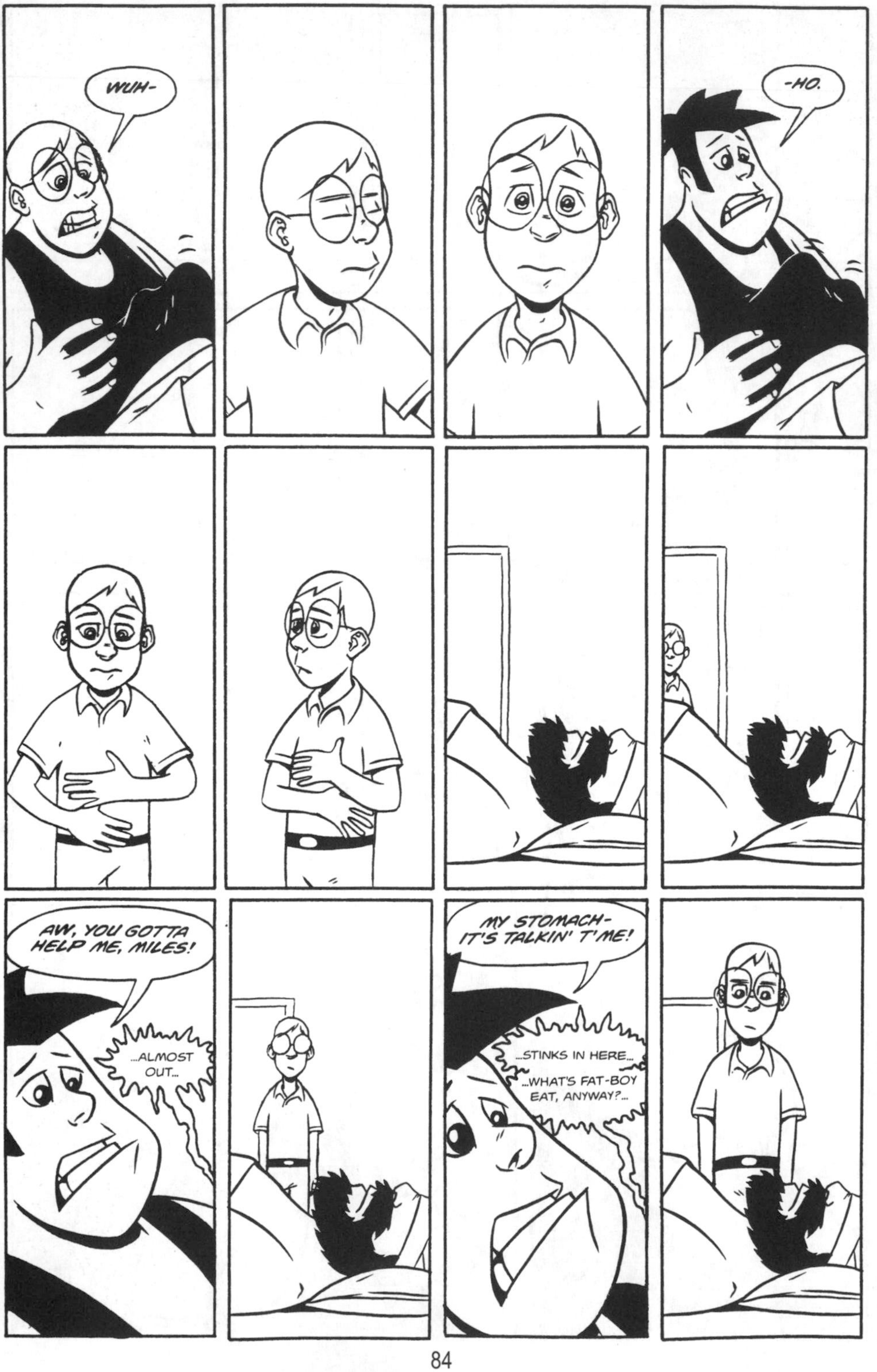
WUH-
-HO.
AW, YOU GOTTA HELP ME, MILES!
...ALMOST OUT...
MY STOMACH- IT'S TALKIN' T'ME!
...STINKS IN HERE...
...WHAT'S FAT-BOY EAT, ANYWAY?...

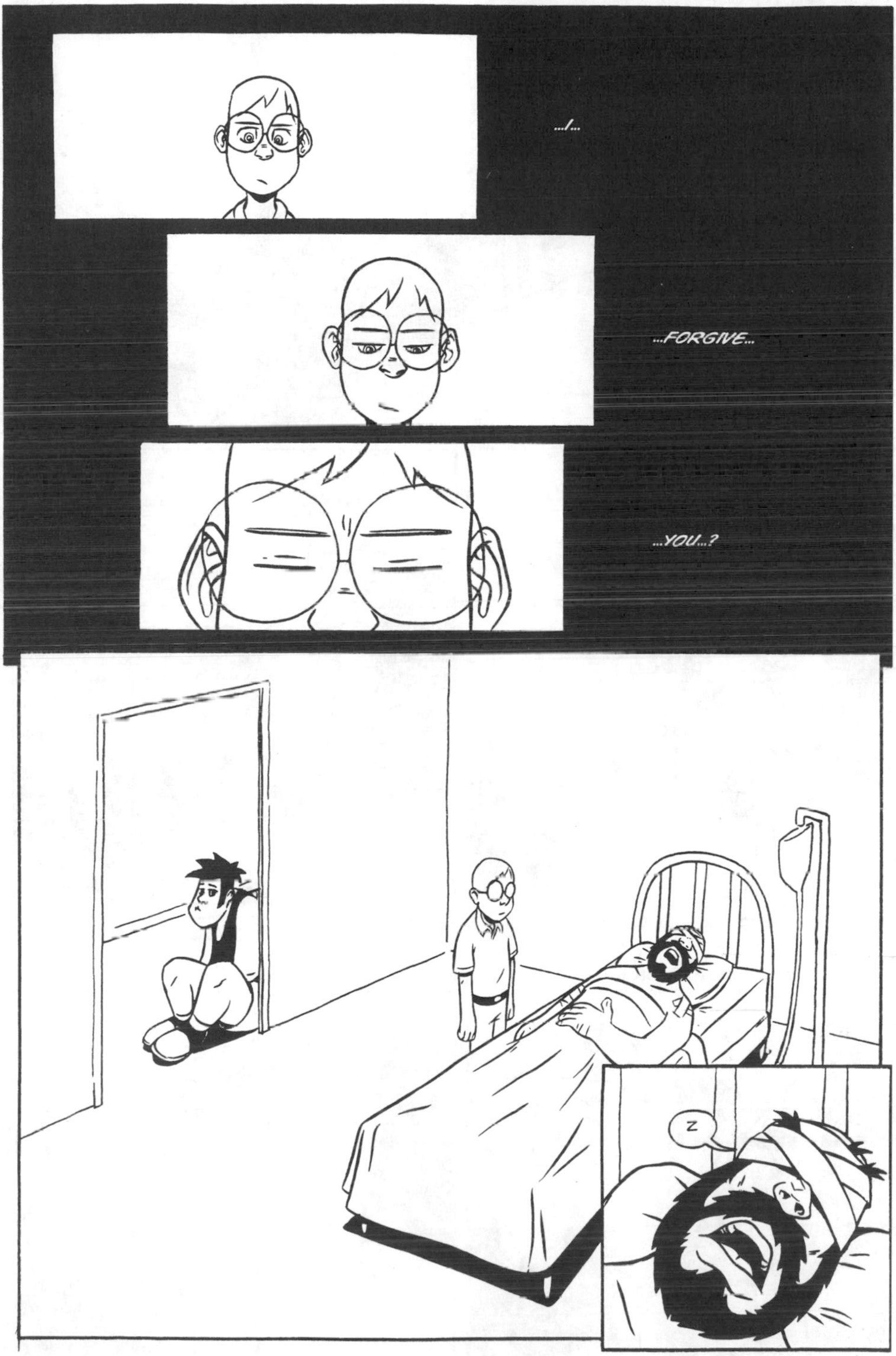
...I...
...FORGIVE...
...YOU...?
Z

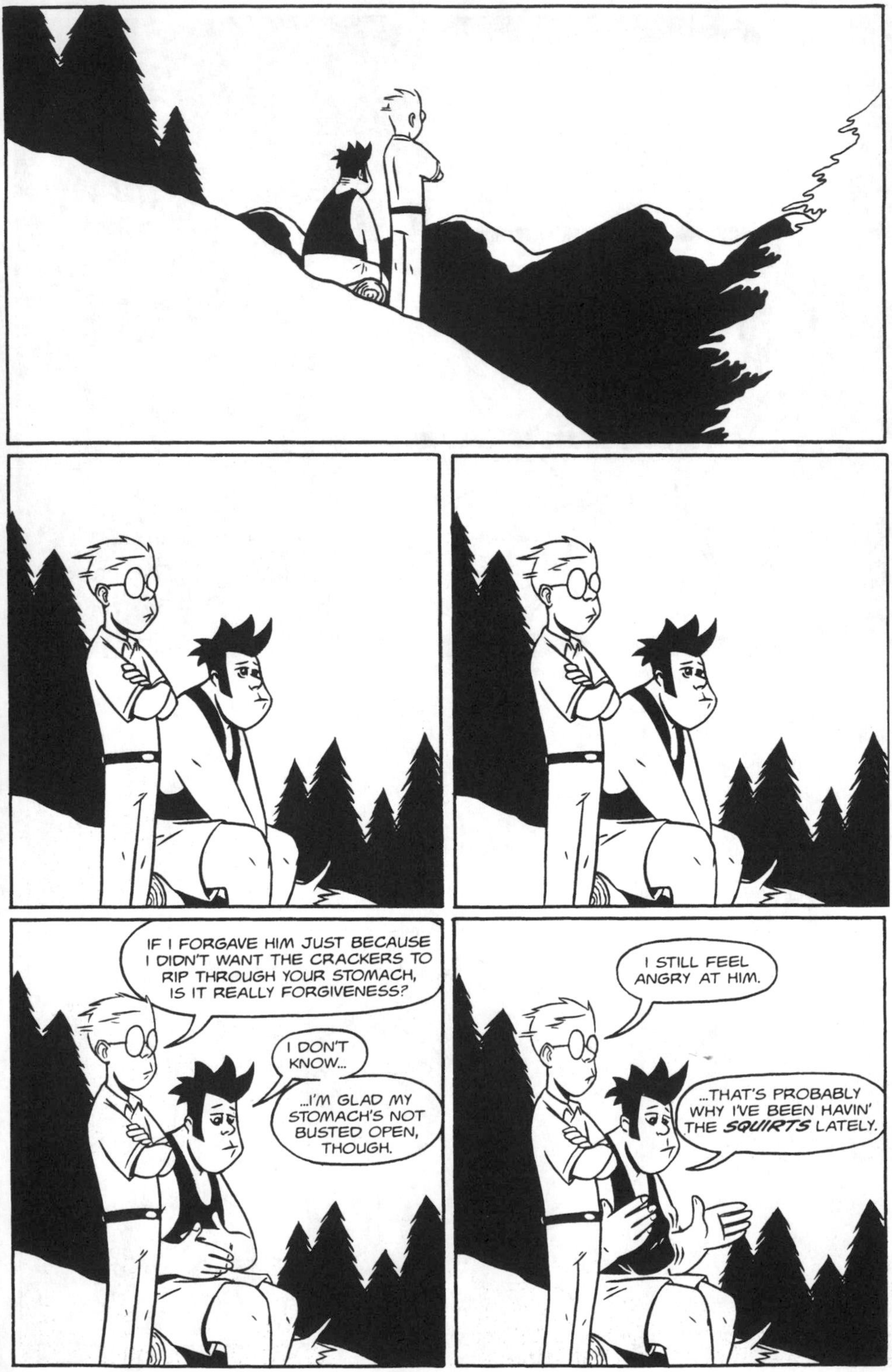
IF I FORGAVE HIM JUST BECAUSE I DIDN'T WANT THE CRACKERS TO RIP THROUGH YOUR STOMACH, IS IT REALLY FORGIVENESS?
I DON'T KNOW...
...I'M GLAD MY STOMACH'S NOT BUSTED OPEN, THOUGH.
I STILL FEEL ANGRY AT HIM.
...THAT'S PROBABLY WHY I'VE BEEN HAVIN' THE *SQUIRTS* LATELY.

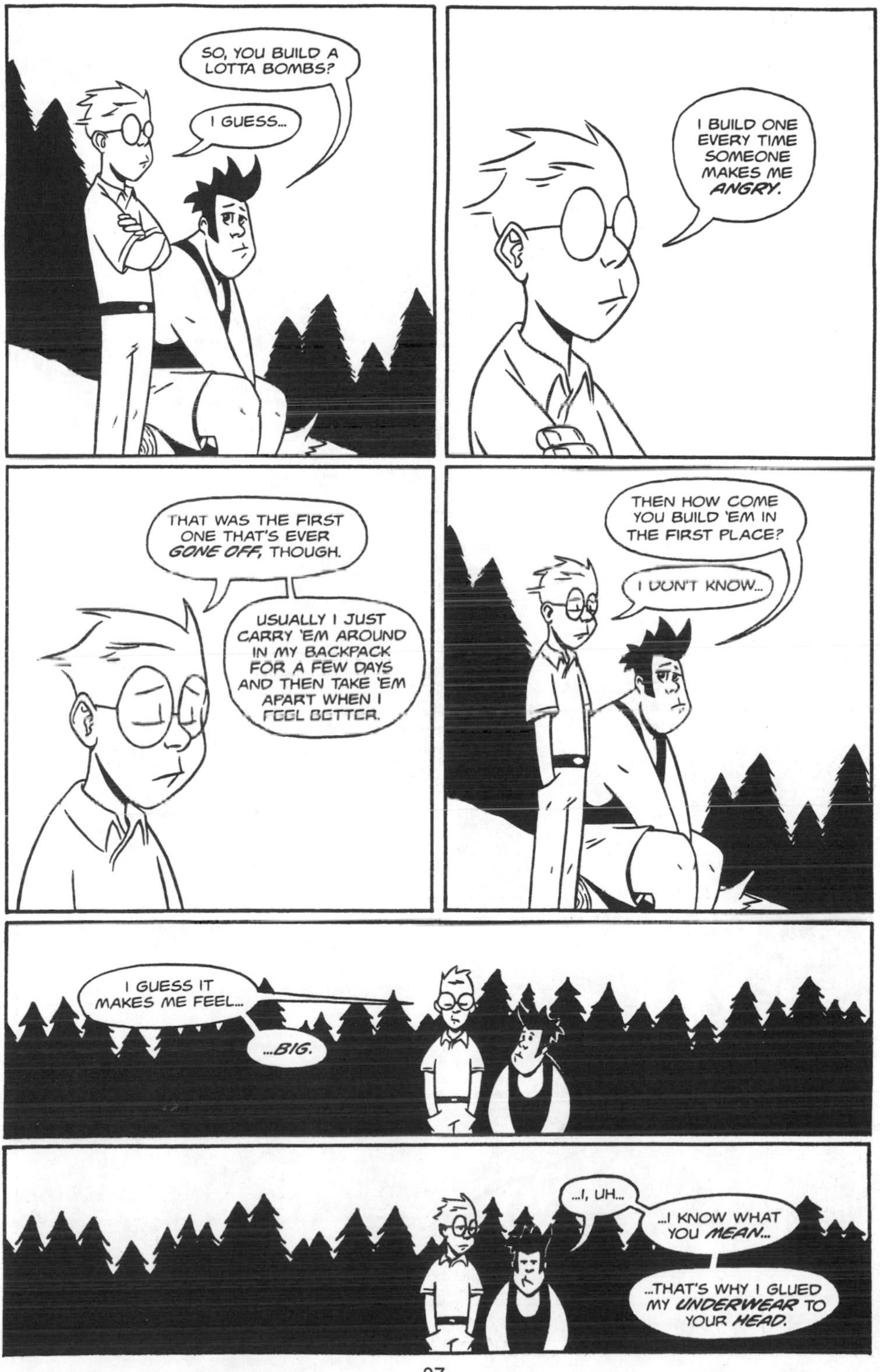
SO, YOU BUILD A LOTTA BOMBS?
I GUESS...
I BUILD ONE EVERY TIME SOMEONE MAKES ME ANGRY.
THAT WAS THE FIRST ONE THAT'S EVER GONE OFF, THOUGH.
USUALLY I JUST CARRY 'EM AROUND IN MY BACKPACK FOR A FEW DAYS AND THEN TAKE 'EM APART WHEN I FEEL BETTER.
THEN HOW COME YOU BUILD 'EM IN THE FIRST PLACE?
I DON'T KNOW...
I GUESS IT MAKES ME FEEL...
...BIG.
...I, UH...
...I KNOW WHAT YOU MEAN...
...THAT'S WHY I GLUED MY UNDERWEAR TO YOUR HEAD.

SAMMY
THE BAKER
AND THE M.A.C

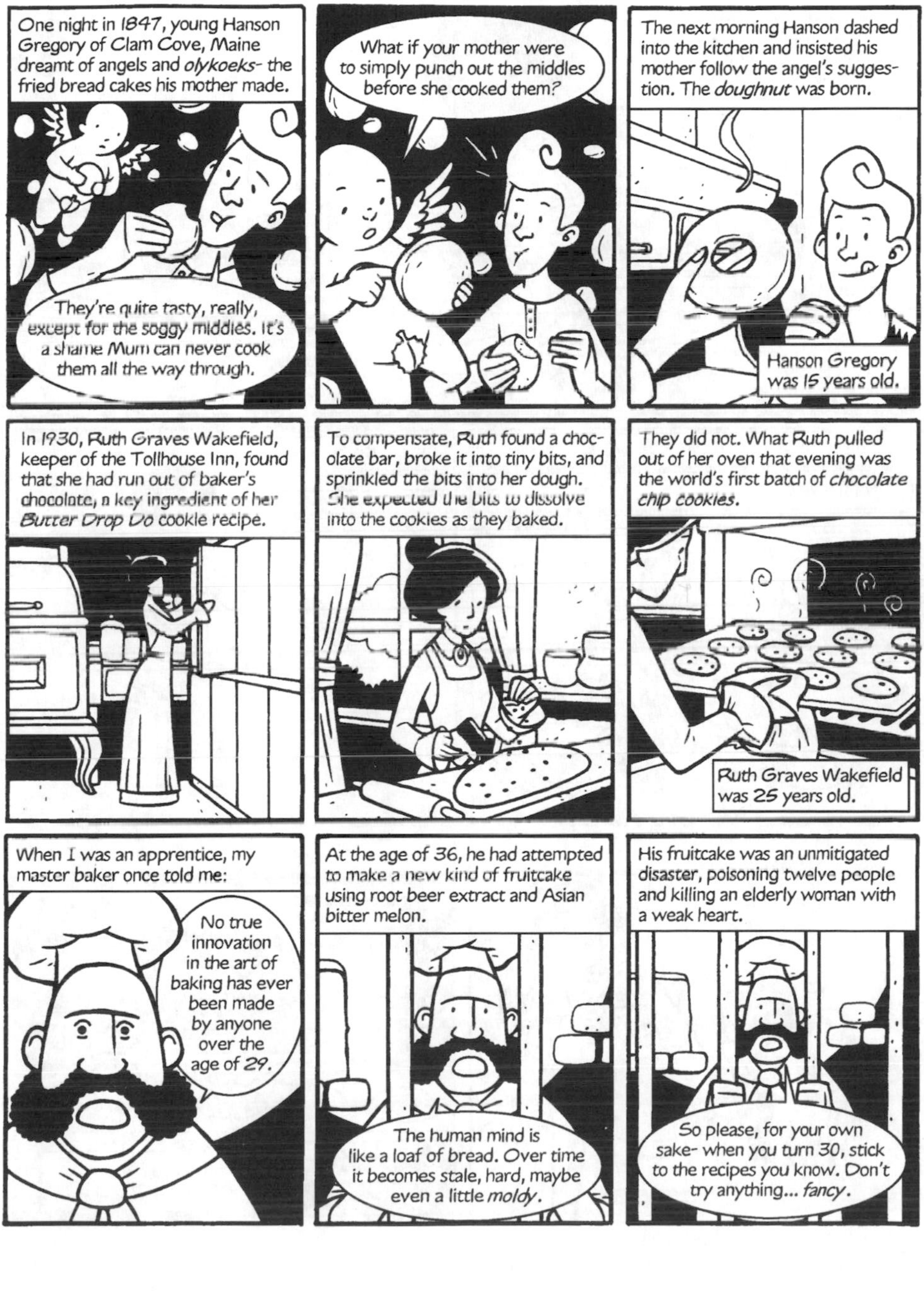

One night in 1847, young Hanson Gregory of Clam Cove, Maine dreamt of angels and *olykoeks*- the fried bread cakes his mother made.
They're quite tasty, really, except for the soggy middles. It's a shame Mum can never cook them all the way through.
What if your mother were to simply punch out the middles before she cooked them?
The next morning Hanson dashed into the kitchen and insisted his mother follow the angel's suggestion. The *doughnut* was born.
Hanson Gregory was 15 years old.
In 1930, Ruth Graves Wakefield, keeper of the Tollhouse Inn, found that she had run out of baker's chocolate, a key ingredient of her *Butter Drop Do* cookie recipe.
To compensate, Ruth found a chocolate bar, broke it into tiny bits, and sprinkled the bits into her dough. She expected the bits to dissolve into the cookies as they baked.
They did not. What Ruth pulled out of her oven that evening was the world's first batch of *chocolate chip cookies*.
Ruth Graves Wakefield was 25 years old.
When I was an apprentice, my master baker once told me:
No true innovation in the art of baking has ever been made by anyone over the age of 29.
At the age of 36, he had attempted to make a new kind of fruitcake using root beer extract and Asian bitter melon.
The human mind is like a loaf of bread. Over time it becomes stale, hard, maybe even a little *moldy*.
His fruitcake was an unmitigated disaster, poisoning twelve people and killing an elderly woman with a weak heart.
So please, for your own sake- when you turn 30, stick to the recipes you know. Don't try anything... *fancy*.

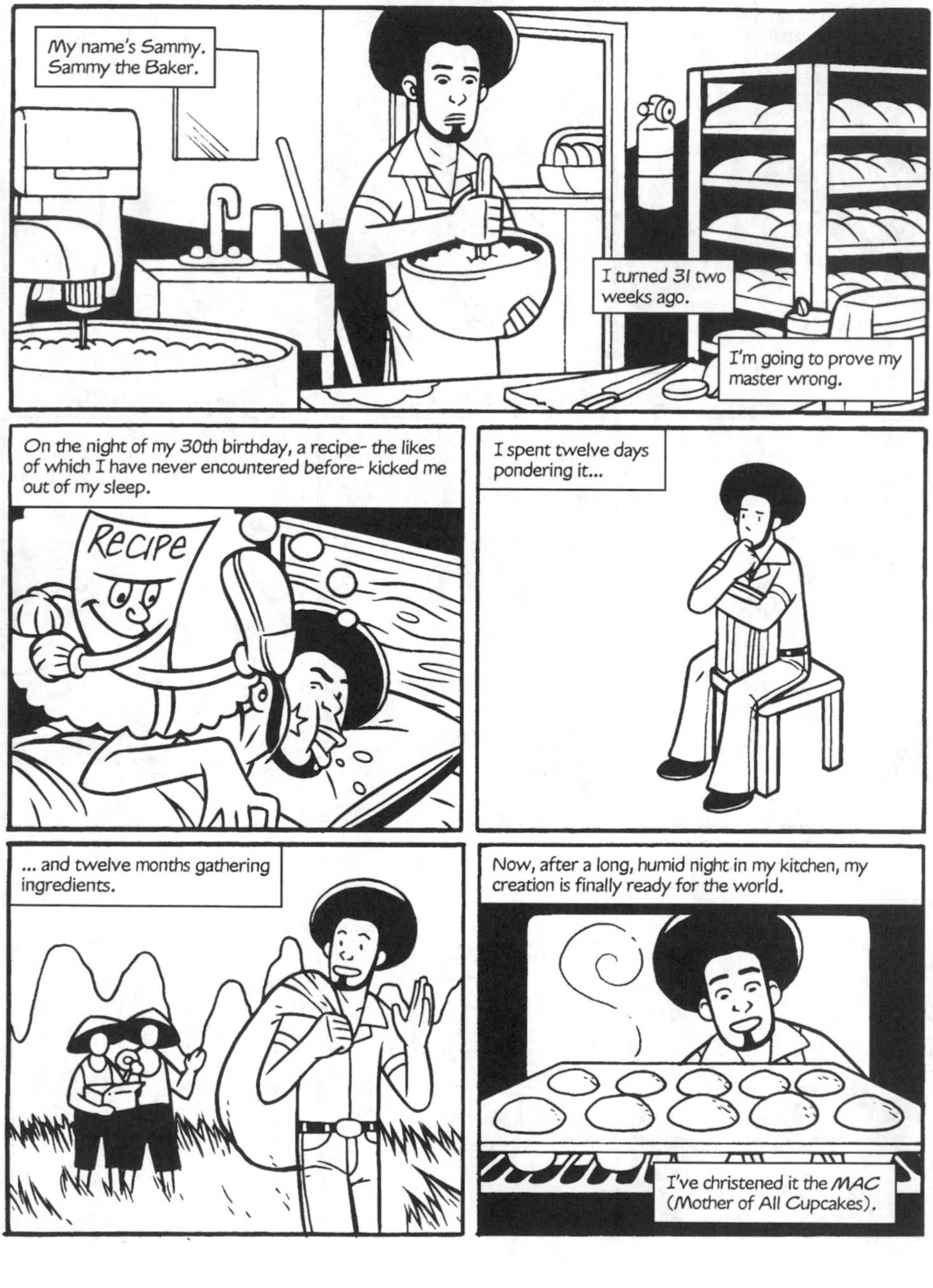
My name's Sammy. Sammy the Baker.
I turned 31 two weeks ago.
I'm going to prove my master wrong.
On the night of my 30th birthday, a recipe- the likes of which I have never encountered before- kicked me out of my sleep.
RECIPE
I spent twelve days pondering it...
... and twelve months gathering ingredients.
Now, after a long, humid night in my kitchen, my creation is finally ready for the world.
I've christened it the *MAC* (Mother of All Cupcakes).

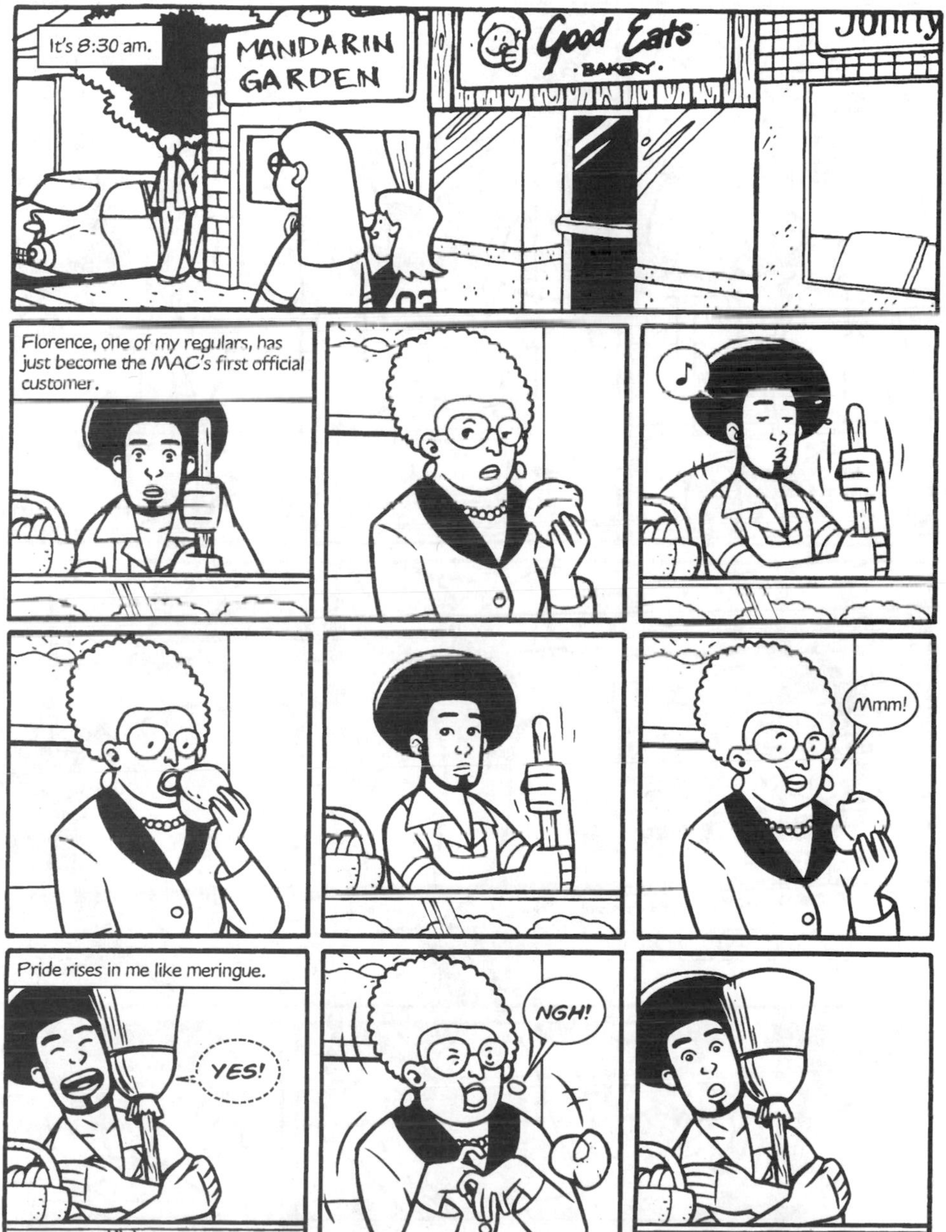
It's 8:30 am.
MANDARIN GARDEN
Good Eats
·BAKERY·
Florence, one of my regulars, has just become the MAC's first official customer.
♪
Mmm!
Pride rises in me like meringue.
YES!
NGH!

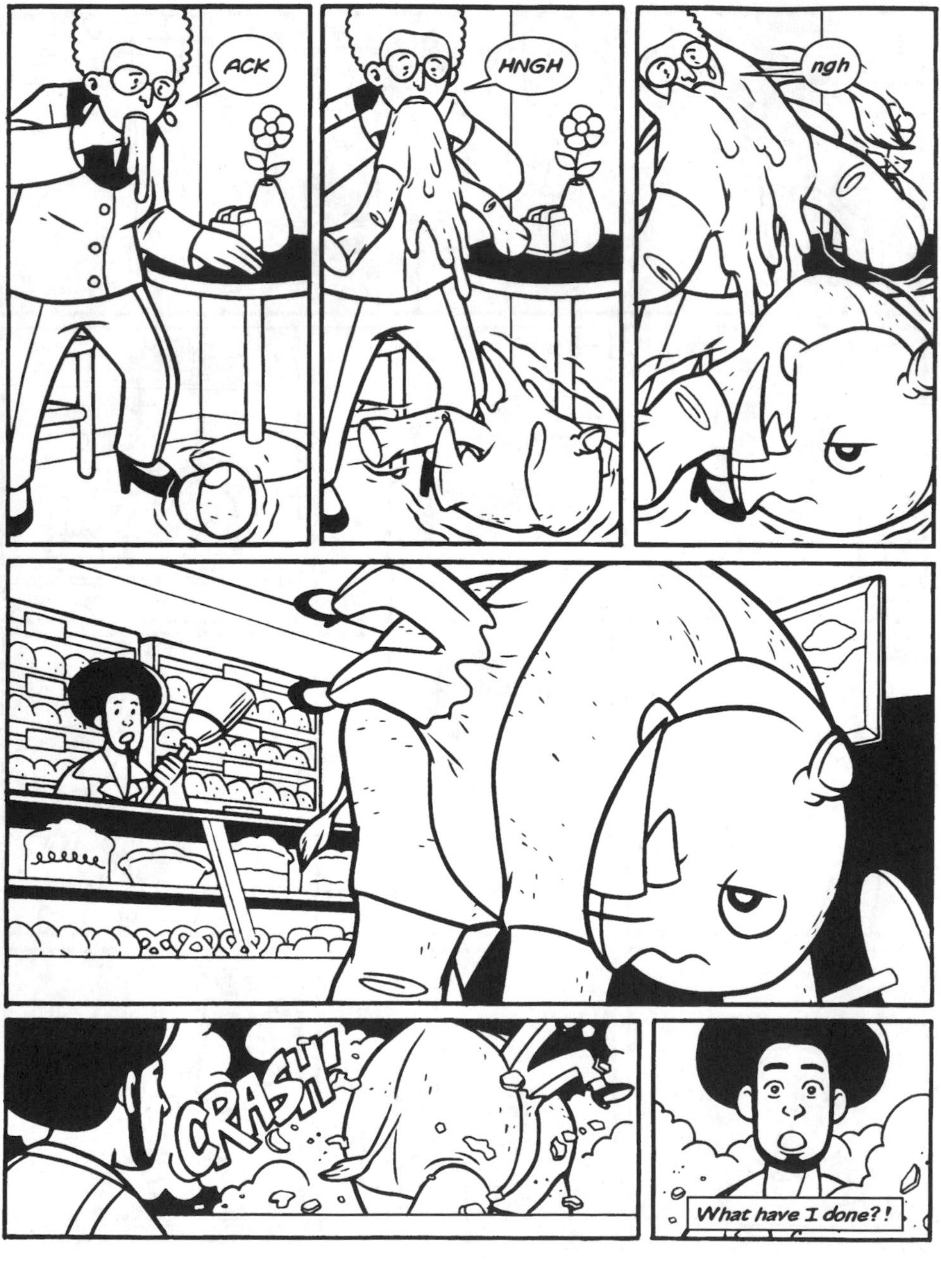
ACK
HNGH
ngh
CRASH!
What have I done?!

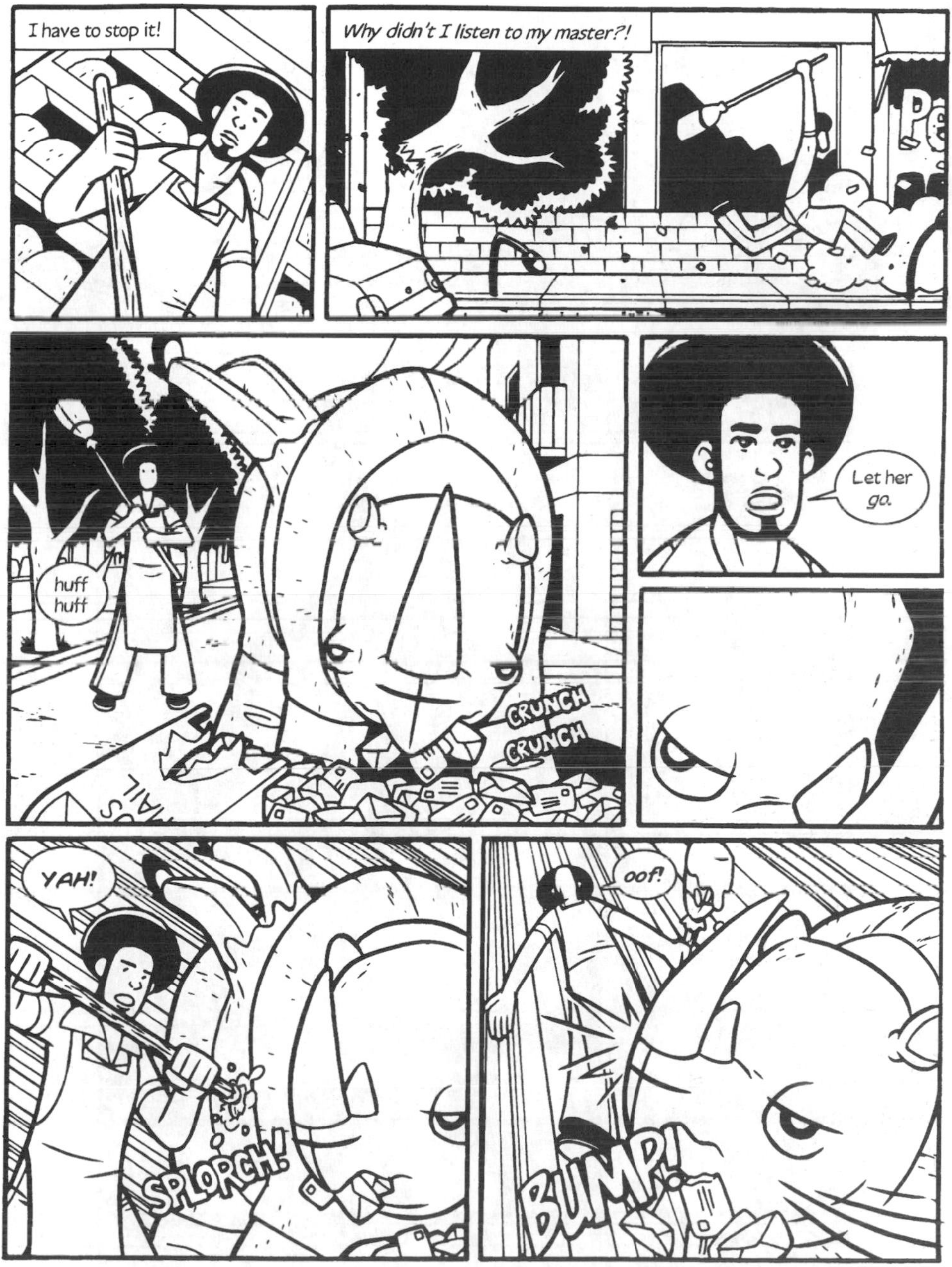
I have to stop it!
Why didn't I listen to my master?!
huff huff
CRUNCH
CRUNCH
Let her go.
YAH!
SPLORCH!
oof!
BUMP!

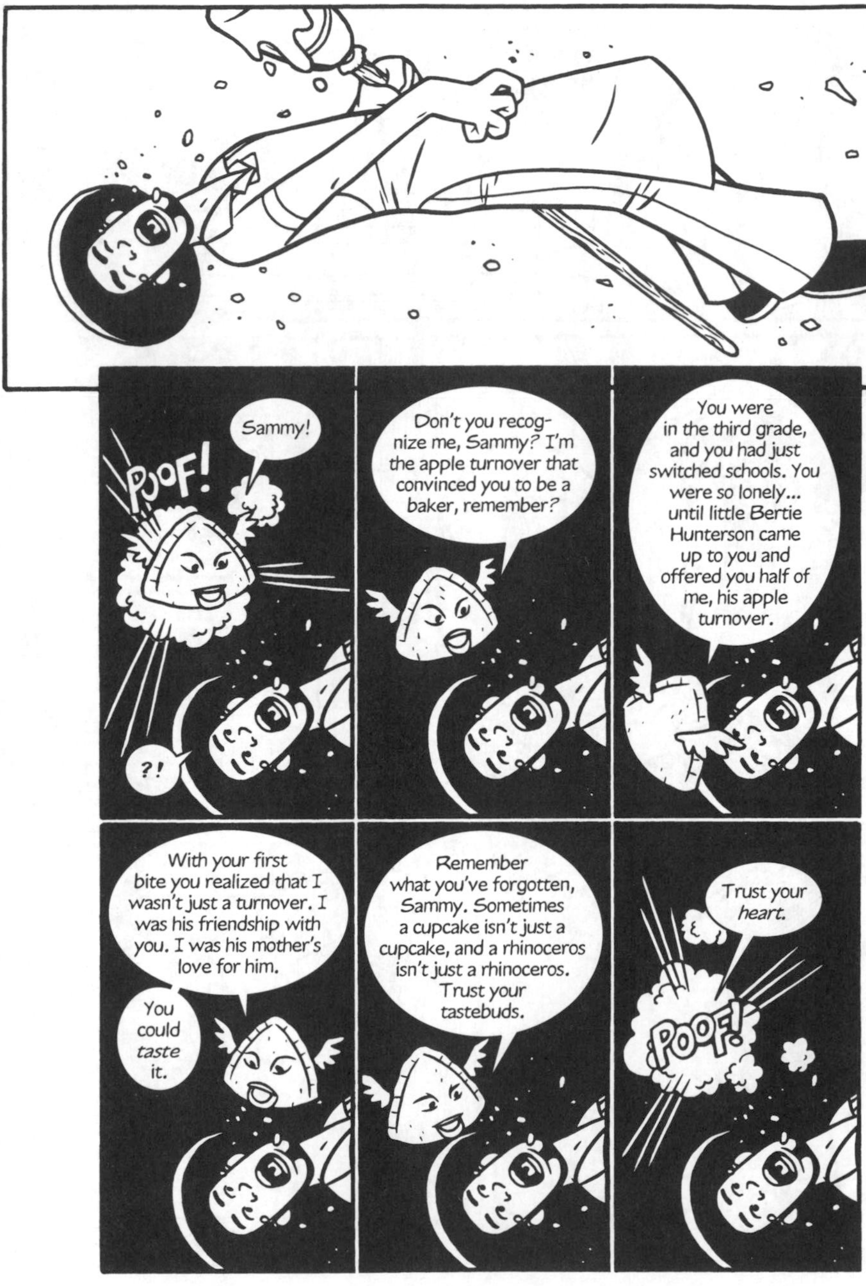
POOF!
Sammy!
?!
Don't you recognize me, Sammy? I'm the apple turnover that convinced you to be a baker, remember?
You were in the third grade, and you had just switched schools. You were so lonely... until little Bertie Hunterson came up to you and offered you half of me, his apple turnover.
With your first bite you realized that I wasn't just a turnover. I was his friendship with you. I was his mother's love for him.
You could *taste* it.
Remember what you've forgotten, Sammy. Sometimes a cupcake isn't just a cupcake, and a rhinoceros isn't just a rhinoceros. Trust your tastebuds.
Trust your *heart.*
POOF!

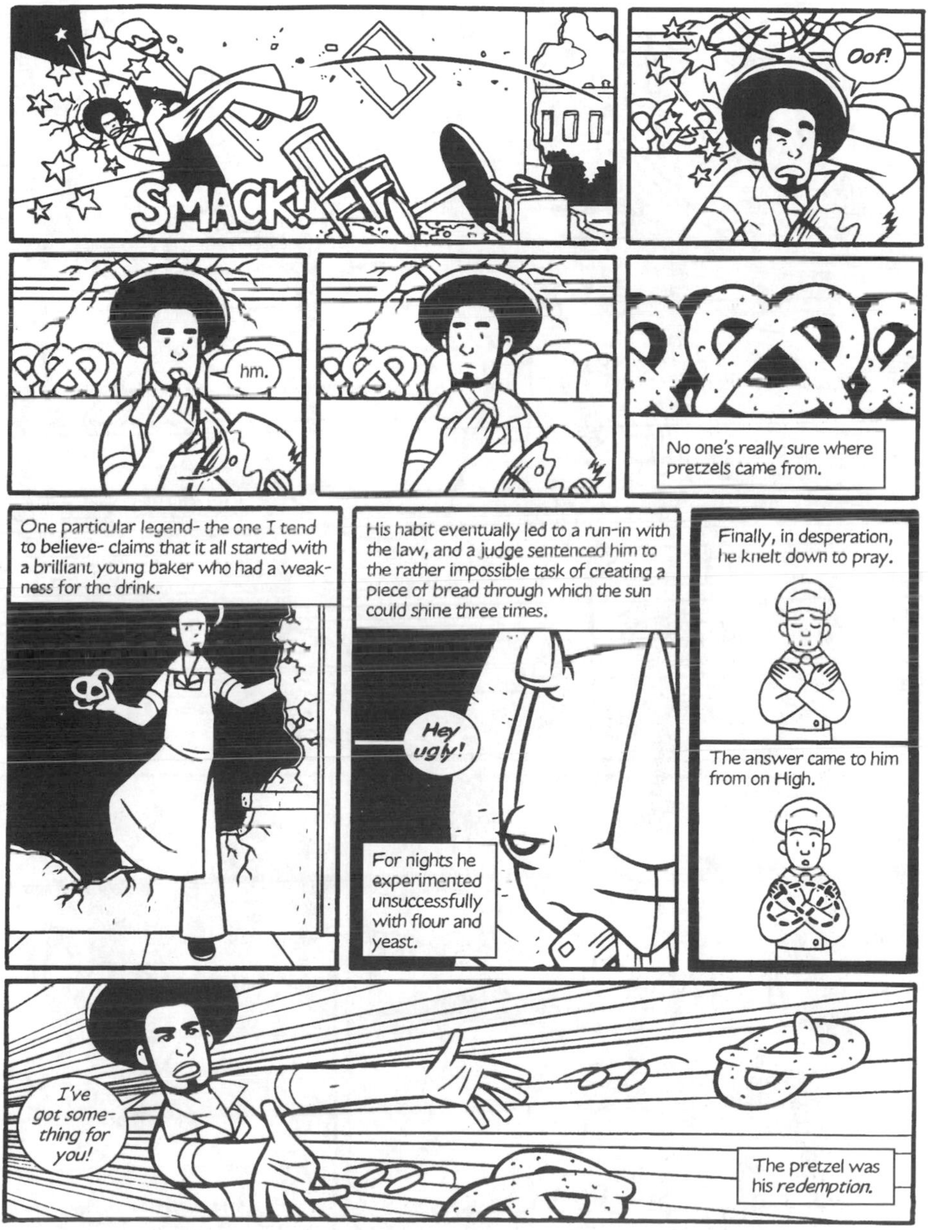
SMACK!
Oof!
hm.
No one's really sure where pretzels came from.
One particular legend- the one I tend to believe- claims that it all started with a brilliant young baker who had a weakness for the drink.
His habit eventually led to a run-in with the law, and a judge sentenced him to the rather impossible task of creating a piece of bread through which the sun could shine three times.
Hey ugly!
For nights he experimented unsuccessfully with flour and yeast.
Finally, in desperation, he knelt down to pray.
The answer came to him from on High.
I've got something for you!
The pretzel was his *redemption.*

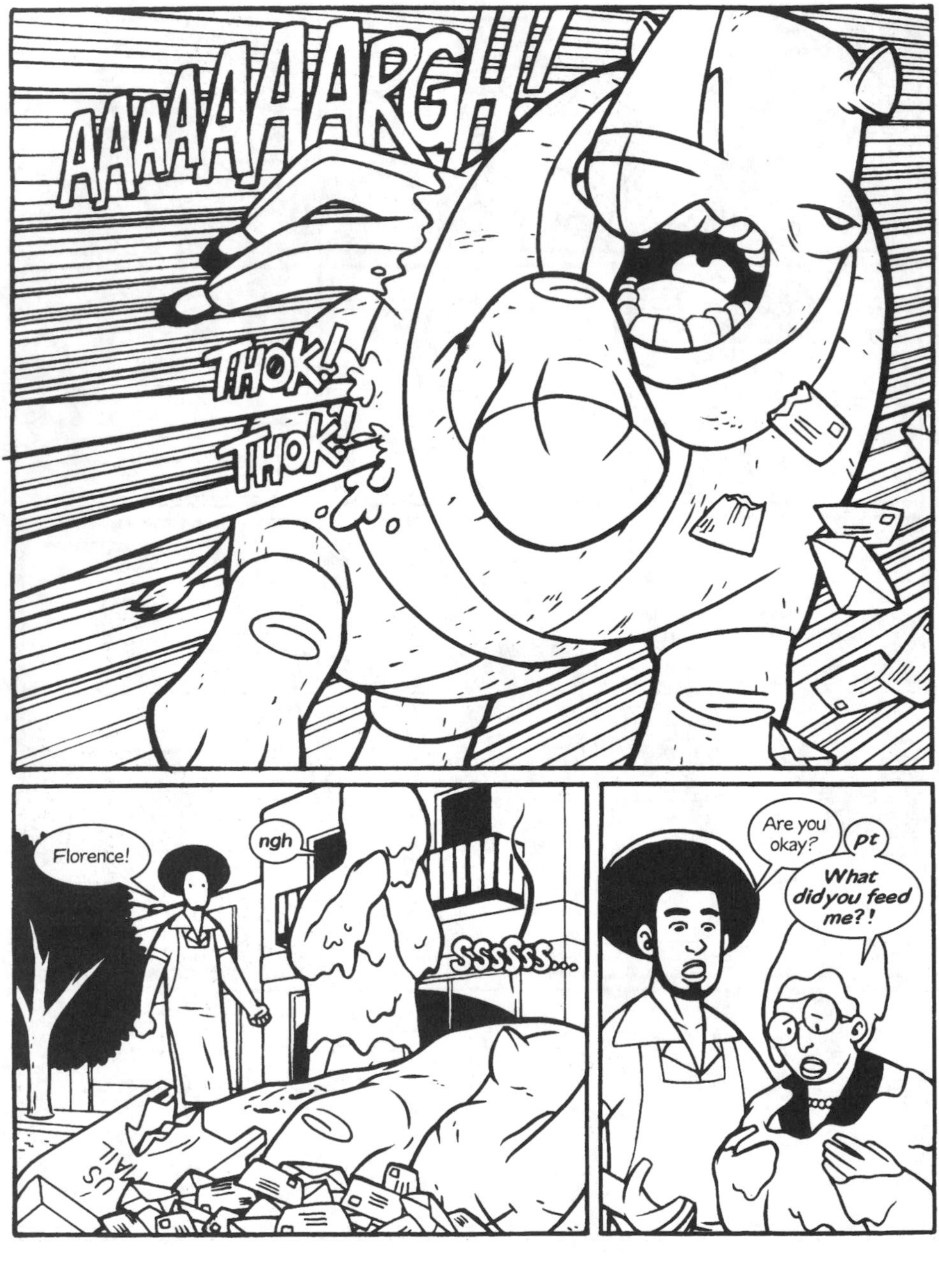
AAAAAAARGH!!
THOK!
THOK!
Florence!
ngh
SSSSSS...
US MAIL
Are you okay?
pt
What did you feed me?!

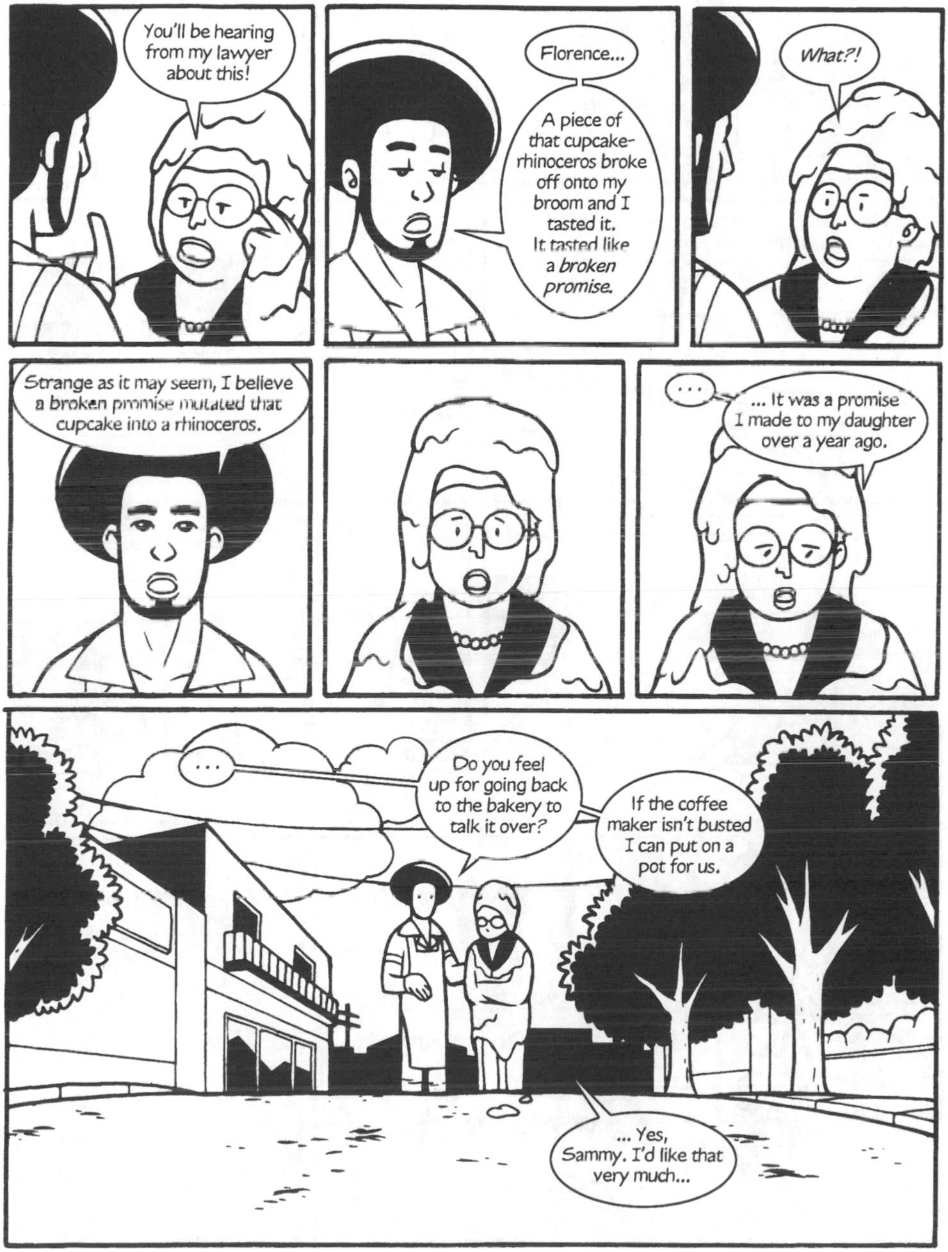
You'll be hearing from my lawyer about this!
Florence...
A piece of that cupcake-rhinoceros broke off onto my broom and I tasted it. It tasted like a *broken promise.*
What?!
Strange as it may seem, I believe a broken promise mutated that cupcake into a rhinoceros.
...
... It was a promise I made to my daughter over a year ago.
...
Do you feel up for going back to the bakery to talk it over?
If the coffee maker isn't busted I can put on a pot for us.
... Yes, Sammy. I'd like that very much...

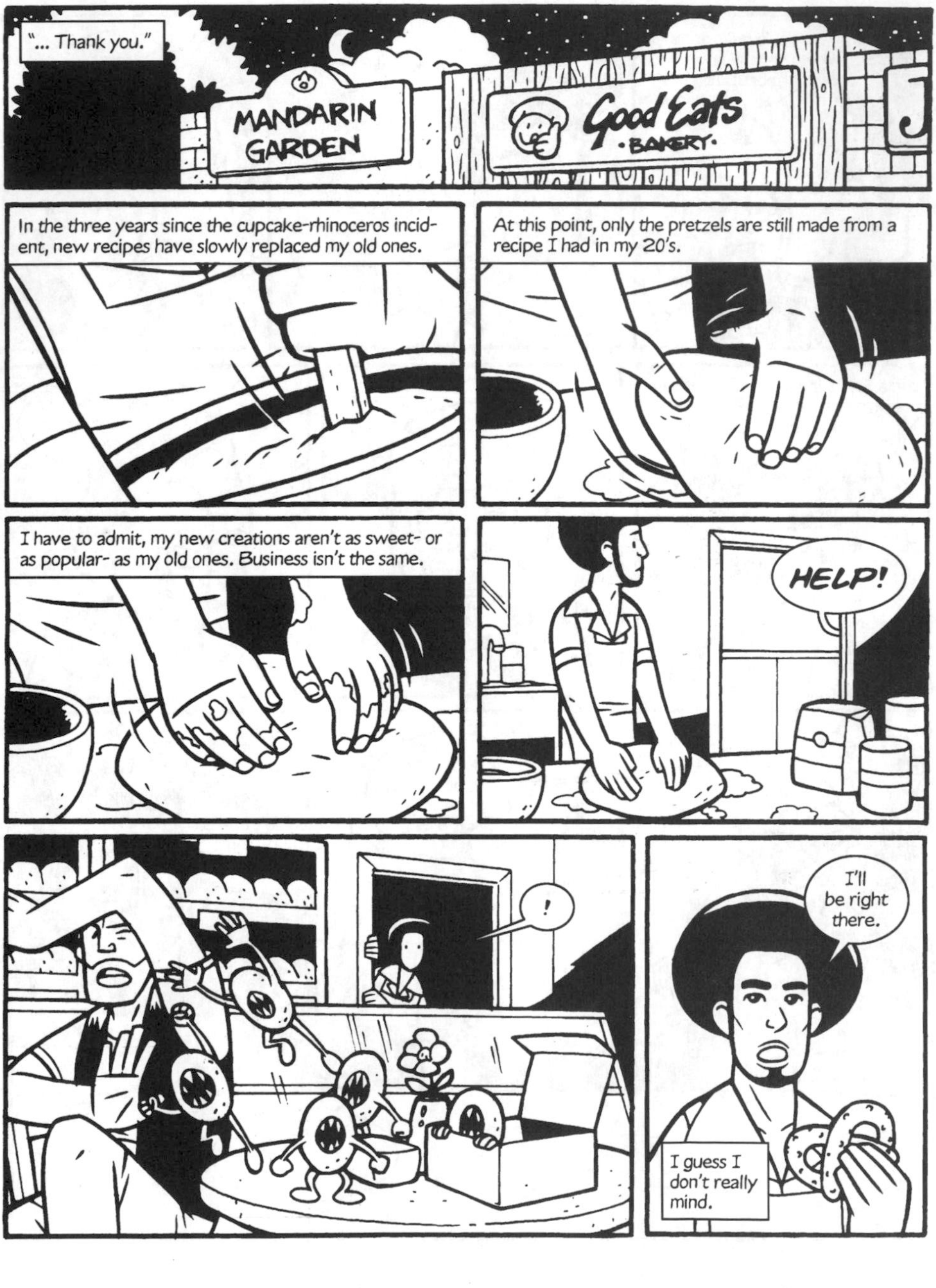
"... Thank you."
MANDARIN GARDEN
Good Eats
·BAKERY·
In the three years since the cupcake-rhinoceros incid-ent, new recipes have slowly replaced my old ones.
At this point, only the pretzels are still made from a recipe I had in my 20's.
I have to admit, my new creations aren't as sweet- or as popular- as my old ones. Business isn't the same.
HELP!
!
I'll be right there.
I guess I don't really mind.